Intro

Aim

The G[...]
signed [...]
the Growing Christians series of daily reading notes.

Each subject in the series follows a thematic approach and has a corresponding set of group materials. These are not designed to be exhaustive but are for the purpose of stimulating discussions and interaction around the truths and concepts that have been followed daily.

The purpose of combining daily reading material together with group study, is not just for a study period, but so that group members might:

- gain a greater appreciation of Biblical facts and truths, stimulating growth and maturity
- develop a daily discipline of reading the Bible
- gain deeper personal relationships
- gain new insights encouraging the practical application of Biblical principles to daily living

What you will need

Each group member will need to have their own set of the daily reading notes (e.g. the book on *Prayer* if this is the theme you are looking at). It is important that each member will have read the first *two weeks* of daily comment and Scripture before your first meeting together.

[...]e group study notes can be photo-[...]ied for each group member. En-[...]e that each of them has a copy of the [...]ropriate session's questions before, [...]at the meeting.

Number and length of meetings

Although the daily readings in the Growing Christians booklets cover seven weeks, the group sessions will only take place over *six weeks*. This is because the first week's readings are treated as an introduction to the theme. There is no specific activity material for this week. The first time your group meets will be *after the second week's readings*. The activities of your first session will relate to that week.

Each group session should take around 45 minutes, depending on how much time is given to the different sections. Seek to pace the group discussions so that you do not get bogged down on one issue.

Using the Leader's Guide

The Leader's Guide is linked to the daily readings through the brief synopsis in the left hand column, which in turn is linked to the verse next to it. The idea of completing the verse is to encourage members to read the truth for themselves. The verse and synopsis form the discussion starter for comments and observations on the daily readings.

The questions and verses that follow are to develop further thinking and discussion, with some of the answers being more obvious than others. This is to encourage the establishing of a stronger Biblical framework of the truth and a deeper understanding, through reflection on what the scripture says. The key is always to relate the question to the heading and synopsis in the left hand column.

For example: In Prayer Session 2 the synopsis entitled *Refocus* speaks of "our busy schedules and activities". The question is asked "What is the tendency in life? Ecclesiastes 2:17–23." Possible answers from the passage are that everything seems pointless or that life becomes a constant round of work and activity where you can hardly stop to think. In the context of the discussion, the second answer is the more relevant one.

There are also exercises to participate in and to encourage personal involvement and sharing in the group. You need only use as much of the material as you think is necessary for a particular session.

Each session concludes with an Action Plan to be implemented during the following week. It is good to start subsequent sessions by discussing how the group got on with their Action Plans – either in twos or threes, or as a whole group. This is a time to encourage any who might be struggling.

At the end of each session make sure you recap to the group, the content of your discussion and any conclusions you may have come to.

Guidelines

1 **Preparation is the key** to any effective study, so aim to spend some time reviewing the study notes and preparing your guiding thoughts prior to each group session.

One way to avoid panic preparation just before the group starts is to spend an extra 15 minutes each day working through the relevant Leader's Guide material at the same time as you read the daily notes in the Growing Christians booklet. You can make a note at this time of your own thoughts and highlight particular things that you feel should be explored and discussed in the group.

2 **Don't lecture** or use the group as an opportunity to air your own views. Instead, encourage individual members to say how they got on with their daily readings and then develop the discussion around the study guide material. Your role is not to dominate, but to lead and encourage participation.

3 **If possible, encourage each member to put aside the same period of time each day** so that the group feel that they are all doing the same thing together each day. The daily readings accompanied by a few minutes' prayer take about 15 minutes.

4 Seek to make allowances for everyone's perspective and don't let more vocal individuals dominate the group. Draw others in by saying, for example, "John, how did you get on with Tuesday's readings?" Develop a sensitivity to one another in the group. Link one person's comments to another's, affirming all of the participants.

5 Don't be side-tracked from the subject of the study. Listen to and encourage each person's insights but keep the discussion on course by saying something like, "That's an interesting perspective, but not really what we are focusing on at the moment." Then draw someone else in by saying, for example, "Helen, what were your thoughts on ...?" and so steer back onto the subject.

6 Look to the Holy Spirit to guide you into truth and to bring you into fresh spiritual insight. If you get stuck on some point, simply stop and ask the Lord for further understanding. Remember, the purpose of the study is to let God speak through His Word.

7 Ask different people in the group to read the Bible passages and references out loud, though be sensitive to any who might find it embarrassing or difficult to read in a group.

8 Don't be frightened of pauses and moments of quietness: people often need this time to think. Sometimes it is good to interject some moments of quiet reflection by suggesting that the group takes a few moments to ponder individually on an issue.

9 Acknowledge all contributions. Never put people down, reject an answer or contradict a group member. Remember, where there is a winner there is always a loser, and no-one likes the feeling of rejection that comes with losing, especially if it is keenly felt in front of others.

Your goal is to win the person, not to alienate them. It is always best to say, "That is one viewpoint that some people hold. However, there is another," and go on to present the other view. In this way it is not a question of "I'm right, you're wrong", but a difference of perspectives. Obviously, differing opinions will be expressed from time to time. This is healthy. However, if the answer or viewpoint is clearly wrong, this should be gently and tactfully pointed out.

10 From time to time, feed back to the group truths you are discovering together and conclusions that you are coming to. This will give opportunity to clarify anything that may not have been expressed too clearly earlier in the discussion.

The Basis of Prayer

Key Truth

"Then Jesus told his disciples a parable to show them that
_____."

Luke 18:1

Most of us want to pray, know that we ought to pray more, but often find it difficult to sustain our prayer lives.

List below the difficulties you find with prayer	Possible solution

SHARE WITH THE GROUP AND TOGETHER MAKE A COMPOSITE LIST OF GOALS TO PURSUE DURING THE SIX WEEK STUDY.

GOALS
_____

_____

_____

_____

Quotes on prayer:

- Prayer is the key of the morning and the bolt of the evening.
- Prayer is two people in love.
- Prayer is conversation with God.
- Prayer is seeing things from God's point of view.
- Prayer is exhaling the spirit of man and inhaling the Spirit of God.
- Prayer is the slender nerve that moves the muscles of divine omnipotence.

Write out your own definition of prayer:
Prayer is:

_____

_____

_____

SHARE YOUR DEFINITIONS WITH THE GROUP.

Why should we pray?

☐ To build a relationship   Add to this list:
☐ To get answers   ☐ _____
☐ To deepen our spirituality   ☐ _____
☐ It's a good discipline   ☐ _____
☐ To bring help to others
☐ To discover the will of God
☐ To get out of trouble
☐ To please God

Consider this list and number it in your own order of priority.

SHARE YOUR CONCLUSIONS IN THE GROUP.

■ What was the disciple's request? *Luke 11:1*

■ What does this imply?

DISCUSS SOME OF THE ELEMENTS THAT ARE PART OF THE LEARNING PROCESS.

What is Prayer?

IT IS CONVERSATION AND COMMUNION WITH GOD, BASED ON THREE KEY ELEMENTS: CO-OPERATION, SURRENDER AND CREATIVITY.

Co-operation

Prayer is co-operation with God. In prayer you align your will, desires, and life to God. You and God become one on the matter of your life plans, goals and desires and you proceed to work them out together.

"This is the confidence we have in approaching God:_____

_____ .

And if we know that he hears us – whatever we ask – we know that we have what we asked of him." 1 John 5:14–15

■ What is the underlying factor that holds the universe together? *John 6:38*

■ What prayer did Jesus repeat three times? *Matthew 26:36–45*

■ How is God's will revealed? *2 Peter 1:20–21*

■ What does Jesus teach His disciples to pray? *Matthew 6:10*

DISCUSS WHAT IS THE IMPLICATION OF THIS TRUTH?

Surrender

Once we recognise that the heart of prayer is bringing God's will into the world, we need to recognise that we must surrender

"... we have confidence before God and receive from him anything we ask, because _____

_____ ." 1 John 3:21b–22

■ What militates against surrender? *James 4:1–3*

■ What attitude should we take? *Philippians 2:3–11*

■ What is the key to surrender? *1 Corinthians 8:6*

our own pur-
poses, plans,
will and desires
into His hands.

Word Study

LORD: Kurios – κύριος (Greek)
One who has supreme authority and has
dominion and rule over their subjects.

DISCUSS WHAT DO YOU UNDERSTAND "THE
LORDSHIP OF CHRIST" TO MEAN?

Creativity

**Prayer is often
described as a
birth process.
As we surrender
our will and
desires to
His higher
purposes,
through our
prayers they
are brought
into being.
This is an
exciting dimen-
sion of prayer.
God's creativity
births His
purposes over
the bridge of
our prayer.**

"If you remain in me _____ ,
ask whatever you wish, and it will be given you." John 15:7

■ What is the basis of faith? *Romans 10:17*

■ What is the result of faith exercised in prayer?
Matthew 21:22

■ In what way was Job's prayer creative? *Job 42:7–10*

 ## Practical Tip

When praying a prayer of surrender, lift up
your hands, as a physical act of surrender.

ANSWER BEFORE SOMETHING FIRST EXISTS IN
REALITY, E.G., A BUILDING, WHERE DOES IT
"EXIST"? HOW CAN WE RELATE THIS TO PRAYER?

Action Plan

During the next week list ten things you know to be the
will of God, e.g. that all might be saved. Make a second list
of your own prayer requests, e.g. that my dad might be
saved.

Match together those that are compatible, e.g. that all
might be saved, and I would like my dad to be saved. Begin
to pray with faith and confidence about them.

Recap

Prayer is the process whereby we co-operate with God's
will, surrender our will and desires to His purposes, and
allow Him to creatively bring them to birth in our praying.

The Dynamics of Prayer

Key Truth

"Then you will call upon me and come and pray to me, and I will listen to you. _____

_____."

Jeremiah 29:12–13

Explore how you got on with your action plan. Share with anyone who struggled, help them to understand the concept and encourage them to try again.

The question we are looking at this week is what happens to us when we pray. Not only are we bringing God's purposes into being, which we looked at last week, but in the process God Himself impacts our own souls.

Resources

When we pray a transfusion of divine life enters into our souls; we experience a renewal of resources.

"He is before all things, _____

_____."

Colossians 1:17

READ EPHESIANS 1:16–19

Key words	Define these key words
Spirit of wisdom and *revelation*	
That you may *know* him better	

Key words	Define these key words
Eyes of your heart *enlightened*	
The *hope* to which he has called you	
The riches of his glorious *inheritance in* the saints	
His incomparably great *power*	

ASK YOURSELF HOW DO THESE RESOURCES RELATE TO THE DAILY ROUTINES OF LIFE?

Refocus

When we pray we withdraw from our busy schedules and activities. We are able to look at our lives again in the light of our Saviour and gain a new perspective.

"Therefore, holy brothers, who share in the heavenly calling,

_____ *,*

the apostle and high priest whom we confess." Hebrews 3:1

■ See if someone in the group can quote the words of the chorus that starts, "Turn your eyes upon Jesus". Teach it to the group.

■ What is the tendency in life? *Ecclesiastes 2:17–23*

List ten major things that your life focuses on:

_____	_____
_____	_____
_____	_____
_____	_____

■ What do we find most difficult to do? *Psalm 46:10*

List ten things that constantly call for your attention:

_____

_____

_____

_____

_____

_____

_____

_____

_____

_____

■ What was Moses' experience when he took time alone with God? *Exodus 34:29–35*

CHALLENGE DO PEOPLE RECOGNISE A DIFFERENCE IN YOU AFTER PRAYER?

Reality

Prayer is not just a psychological experience. It is the reality of putting us in touch with God Himself.

"These are a shadow of the things that were to come; _____

_____ *."*

Colossians 2:17

■ Where does prayer direct our minds? *Colossians 3:1–10*

■ What brings transformation? *Romans 12:2*

■ What do we receive? *1 Corinthians 2:12–16*

DISCUSS HOW DO ETERNAL REALITIES DIFFER FROM THE WORLD IN WHICH WE LIVE?

Practical Tip

In your imagination put an empty jar on a high shelf, take the thoughts running round in your mind and put them in one by one, now allow God's thoughts to come into your mind.

Relationship

Prayer is communion and time spent in relationship with the One we love.

" ' _____ , *though the world does not know you,* _____ , *and they know that you have sent me.' "* John 17:25

■ Why is prayer an important part of "remaining"? *John 15:1–10*

■ How did Jesus describe His relationship with the Father? *John 8:27–30*

■ What is Jesus' desire for His followers? *John 17:25–26*

Word Study

REMAIN: Menō – μένω (Greek)
To continue in a given place, to dwell permanently, to abide.

Action Plan

Take the two lists you have drawn up and during the week seek to re-prioritise them in relation to prayer.

Recap

As we pray, we draw fresh resources from God, and refocus our lives with the reality of the presence of Jesus, deepening our relationship with Him.

Good Foundations

Key Truth

" 'The rain came down, the streams rose, and the winds blew and beat against that house; yet it did not fall, _____ .' "

Matthew 7:25

SHARE HOW YOU GOT ON WITH YOUR ACTION PLAN.

Most people struggle with prayer, not because they do not have a desire to pray, but because they never take time to establish a workable framework for their prayer life. This week we want to look at some basic building blocks.

Personal Faith

Our first faltering prayer is spoken when we come and repent of our sins and receive God's forgiveness.

"And without faith it is impossible to please God, _____

_____

_____

and that he rewards those who earnestly seek him."
Hebrews 11:6

■ How should we approach God? *Hebrews 4:16*

■ What is the first prayer we should ever pray?
Luke 15:18–19

■ What is the second prayer we should pray?
Matthew 14:30

TO APPLY MAKE SURE THESE PRAYERS ARE PART OF YOUR EXPERIENCE.

Establish a Time

It is better to begin with a little amount of time and then to increase it.

"_____,
and a season for every activity under heaven ..."
Ecclesiastes 3:1

■ What is a good time to pray? *Psalm 5:1–3; Mark 1:35*

■ What are we to do with time? *Ephesians 5:15–20*

■ What does a drunk man do? *Ephesians 5:15–20*

■ What does being filled with the Spirit relate to? *Ephesians 5:15–20*

TALK THROUGH SHARE TOGETHER THE DIFFICULTIES YOU HAVE IN FINDING TIME TO PRAY.

Develop a Habit

Psychologists tell us that if we do something regularly for thirty days it forms a habit.

"*... Continue* _____
with fear and trembling ... " Philippians 2:12b

■ Was Jesus a man of habit? *Luke 4:16; Luke 22:39–41*

QUOTE "IF YOU ARE TOO BUSY TO PRAY, THEN YOU ARE JUST TOO BUSY."

Word Study

TIME:
Chronos – χρόνος **(Greek)**
A space in time; a duration of time; the order and chronology of time.
Kairos – καιρός **(Greek)**
A period of specific opportunity, possibly never to be repeated; the opportune moment.

Practical Tip

Better to start with 1 minute and be motivated than 1 hour and be discouraged.

Time Chart

HOURS	MON	TUES	WED	THURS	FRI	SAT	SUN
am 12-6							
6-7							
7-8							
8-9							
9-10							
10-11							
11-12							
pm 12-1							
1-2							
2-3							
3-4							
4-5							
5-6							
6-7							
7-8							
8-9							
9-10							
10-12							

The purpose of this exercise is to help you to see where your time is spent in an average week. Fill in the spaces indicating exactly what you did for each hour period, (draw a larger chart or enlarge on a photocopier if you need more space). When complete seek to establish regular times of prayer in your schedule. Break down into twos and talk through your chart.

Establish a Place

Try and ensure that it is as favourable as possible – private, quiet, comfortable and conducive to prayer.

" '... when you pray, _____
_____
_____ .

Then your Father, who sees what is done in secret, will reward you.' " Matthew 6:6

■ Where did Jesus often pray? *Luke 5:16; Luke 9:28; Matthew 26:36*

List:

Possible places where you can pray	Possible distractions to eliminate

SHARE **REFLECT YOUR CONCLUSIONS TO THE GROUP, AND WHICH PLACE YOU THINK YOU MIGHT CHOOSE TO PRAY REGULARLY.**

Action Plan

Choose one of the places, decide how much time you will spend praying and establish from your time chart the appropriate time of the day for you. Follow through every day this coming week.

Recap

Prayer starts with salvation and needs to be continued. Choosing a particular time and conducive place, with a commitment to keep your appointment daily, will produce a lifelong habit.

Steps to Follow

Key Truth

"... 'Lord, _____

_____ .' "

Luke 11:1b

SHARE HOW YOU GOT ON WITH YOUR ACTION PLAN.

We are so used to talking that it is important when we are in God's presence to listen to Him and allow Him to talk to us. Life is so busy that the first thing we need to do is establish prayer times. This week we begin looking at some practical steps.

Step 1: A Place of Rest

The old Quakers used to call this "settling down in God".

" *'Come to me, all you who are weary and burdened,* ___

_____ .' "

Matthew 11:28

■ What did the psalmist say? *Psalm 62:1*

■ What can we expect as we wait on God? *Isaiah 40:29–31*

Practical Tip

Often the body is full of tension. Sit and relax for a few moments, allowing your body to go limp like a rag doll. Take some slow, deliberate, deep breaths, and allow your body tension to be released.

Step 2: Meditate on God's Word

Prime the pump of prayer by reading and meditating on Scripture.

" _____

I delight in your decrees; I will not neglect your word."
Psalm 119:15–16

Word Study

MEDITATION:
Hâgâh (Hebrew)
To murmur (in pleasure); to ponder. Psalm 1:2
Sîychâh (Hebrew)
Reflect with deep devotion; to contemplate.
Psalm 119:99
Higgâyôwn (Hebrew)
A musical notation; a murmuring sound.
Psalm 19:14
Meletaō – μελετάω (Greek)
To ponder carefully with the mind; to muse
upon. I Timothy 4:15

■ From this word study write out your own definition of meditation:

_____

_____

Practical Tip

Begin with the Psalms, they tend to be more devotional

■ What did God promise Joshua? *Joshua 1:8*

■ What opportunity to meditate do we **all** have?
Psalm 63:5–6

DISCUSS THE DIFFERENCE BETWEEN BIBLICAL
MEDITATION AND OTHER FORMS OF MEDITATION.

Step 3: Respond to the Challenge

Confess any spiritual violation to God and ask for forgiveness.

■ What four things is Scripture profitable for? *2 Timothy 3:16*

_____

_____

_____

SUMMARISE WHAT DOES THIS MEAN?

■ What did the psalmist do? *Psalm 119:11*

■ What is a prerequisite for answered prayer? *1 John 3:21*

■ What ability does God's Word have? *Hebrews 4:12*

Step 4: Thanksgiving and Praise

Take time to thank God for His goodness and rejoice in your salvation.

"Enter his gates _____

_____ ;

give thanks to him and praise his name." Psalm 100:4

Word Study

PRAISE:
Hâlal (Hebrew)
Expressing gratitude and wonder with our whole being.
Bârak (Hebrew)
Blessing and adoration. Everything belongs to God, therefore nothing should be received without returning a blessing.
Humneō – ὑμνέω (Greek)
A joyful vocal expression that rises from within, lifting you above your circumstances.

PAUSE FOR PRAISE SHARE TOGETHER THINGS YOU CAN GIVE THANKS TO GOD FOR, AND SPEND FIVE TO TEN MINUTES TOGETHER THANKING AND PRAISING HIM.

Step 5: Open Up to God's Spirit

Allow the flow of God's Spirit to come upon you.

"In the same way, the Spirit helps us in our weakness. We do not know what we ought to pray for, _____

_____

with groans that words cannot express." Romans 8:26

■ What does the Holy Spirit bring? *2 Corinthians 3:6; Ezekiel 36:27*

■ What will the Holy Spirit do? *John 16:13–15*

■ What are we to do? *Jude verse 20*

Action Plan

Write a short psalm of thanksgiving during the next week.

Recap

Take moments to rest and relax in God's presence: allow Him to refresh you. Come to His Word, meditate on it and respond to it. Rejoice in His goodness, give Him thanks and allow the Holy Spirit to come upon you and energise you in prayer.

More Steps to Follow

🔑 **Key Truth**

"But as for you, _____
_____ and have become convinced of ..."
2 Timothy 3:14a

READ OUT TO EACH OTHER THE PSALMS YOU
HAVE WRITTEN DURING THE WEEK.

**This week we are moving to the stage of presenting
our requests before the Lord.**

List things that people sometimes do when they pray:

For Example:

Close eyes _____   _____   _____

Kneel down _____   _____   _____

DISCUSS WHICH DO YOU THINK ARE HELPFUL
AND WHY?

Step 6: Come to a Loving Father

**We can never
rise higher in
our under-
standing of
prayer than
our concept of
God.**

" *'This, then, is how you should pray:'* _____
_____ *hallowed be your name ...'* ' "
Matthew 6:9

■ How are we to view God? *Matthew 7:7–11;
Deuteronomy 32:6*

- Why is this difficult for some? *Psalm 27:10; Psalm 68:5*

- What picture did Jesus give in His parable? *Luke 15:19–24*

TALK ABOUT THE CHARACTERISTICS OF FATHERHOOD IN THIS PARABLE.

Step 7: Make Your Requests Known

Be specific in asking God for those things in line with His will.

"Do not be anxious about anything, but in everything, _____ _____, with thanksgiving, _____."

Philippians 4:6

- How are we to ask? *John 15:16*

- What did Jesus promise? *John 16:19–24*

 Practical Tip
Write your requests down on paper. You can then look later at what still needs prayer and what has been answered.

- What are three key words? *Luke 11:1–13*

- What has God promised to supply? *Philippians 4:19*

 Word Study
NEED: Chreia – χρεία (Greek)
That which is needful to carry out life.

PAUSE FOR PRAYER STOP AND ASK FOR TWO OR THREE REQUESTS TO BE MENTIONED, AND PRAY FOR THEM.

Step 8: Ask with Integrity

So often the prayer of our lips does not match the attitude of our hearts. Our hearts need to be at one with our lips.

"Surely _____ ;
you teach me wisdom in the inmost place." Psalm 51:6

■ What is Pharisaism? *Matthew 6:5–6; 23:27–28*

■ What is it possible to do? *Matthew 15:8*

■ What is "a form of godliness"? *2 Timothy 3:5*

■ How did Jesus illustrate integrity in prayer?
Luke 18:9–14

REPEAT ASK THE GROUP TO REPEAT PSALM 51:6 TOGETHER IN UNISON TWO OR THREE TIMES.

Step 9: Danger of Demandingness

Make sure that your prayer times are not just presenting a shopping list and demanding God to fulfil it.

" 'But seek first _____ ,
and all these things will be given to you as well.' "
Matthew 6:33

■ What are we to seek first? *2 Chronicles 7:14,
Psalm 105:4*

■ What does this parable show us about demandingness?
Luke 15:11–32

Step 10: Listen for Direction

Sometimes God wants us to put legs on our prayers by giving us clear direction on what action we should take.

"As the body without the spirit is dead, so _____ _____ is dead." James 2:26

■ What did Elijah discover? *1 Kings 19:12*

■ What did Samuel struggle with? *1 Samuel 3:4–8*

Practical Tip

Keep a notebook handy.

DISCUSS SOME OF THE WAYS GOD SPEAKS TO US IN ANSWER TO PRAYER.

Action Plan

Keep a diary this week of your requests and prayerfully consider what "legs" you can give to your prayers.

Recap

Prayer is honestly talking to God without demanding from Him. Recognise that we can approach Him as a loving Father. In His presence we can make our requests known, expecting Him to speak to us with clear direction.

Intercession

Key Truth

" '_____ . I am not praying for the world, but for those you have given me, for they are yours.' "
John 17:9

It is impossible to develop a healthy prayer life without giving some attention to the needs of others. The action of focusing our prayers on the needs of others is called intercession and someone has described this ministry as "the crowning ministry of the Christian life".

Praying for the Needs of Others

This focuses on bringing about spiritual change in the lives of those who are in need.

"I looked for a man among them who would build up the wall

_____

so that I would not have to destroy it, but I found none."
Ezekiel 22:30

■ How did Moses intercede for the Children of Israel?
Numbers 14:1–20; Deuteronomy 9:25–29

■ What courageous prayer did Moses pray?
Exodus 32:31–32

■ What can we learn from Moses' example?

Word Study

INTERCEDE: Entunchanō – ἐντυγχάνω (Greek)
To meet with in order to converse, then to plead with the person for or against others.

■ What are some of the categories of people we need to pray for:

For Example:

Missionaries _____ _____ _____

Church leaders _____ _____ _____

Christ our Example

Because Christ trod this path before us we know that He can truly represent us before the Father.

"Therefore I will give him a portion among the great, and he will divide the spoils with the strong, because he poured out his life unto death, and was numbered with the transgressors. For he bore the sin of many, _____ _____ ."
Isaiah 53:12

■ What did Jesus pray? *Luke 23:34; 22:32*

■ What was the heart of Christ's prayer? *John 17*

■ What is Christ doing for us? *Romans 8:34, Hebrews 7:25*

Develop a Prayer List

Compile and keep a list of those people and causes for which you feel a special concern.

"I urge, then, first of all, that requests, prayers, intercession and thanksgiving _____ …"
1 Timothy 2:1

Practical Tip
Regularly send a gift to missionaries. Your intercession for them will be more frequent. Matthew 6:21

Spend a few minutes in quiet prayer and list some names of people.

Personal contacts	People serving the Lord overseas

Break down into twos and share your lists before praying together for the people.

Be Unhurried

Don't rush through a list of names, but spend time on each person.

"I always thank my God _____

_____ *..."* Philemon verse 4

■ What could the psalmists say? *Psalm 131; 46:10*

■ How did Paul demonstrate unhurried intercession? *Colossians 1:3–14*

Be Persistent

As long as you are sure that your prayer is in harmony with God's purposes, never give up.

" 'And will not God bring about justice for his chosen ones,

_____ ?

Will he keep putting them off?' " Luke 18:7

■ What did Paul assure those he wrote to?

Ephesians 1:5–16   Philippians 1:3–7
Colossians 1:3   1 Thessalonians 1:2–3
2 Thessalonians 1:11

■ What did Jesus teach about persistence? *Luke 18:1–8*

Live in Faith, Believing

Intercession is like sowing seeds that need continually watering.

"Let us not become weary in doing good, for at the proper time we will reap a _____ ."
Galatians 6:9

■ What is faith? *Hebrews 11:1*

■ What was Elijah's strength? *James 5:16–18*

Action Plan

Set one of your regular prayer times as solely for the purpose of intercession. Encourage someone else to do the same and form an intercession partnership.

Recap

Intercession is praying for others' needs specifically, following Christ's example. It is regularly, persistently and unhurriedly working through my prayer list, then trusting God in believing faith.

Final Thoughts

Have a look back at the goals you set at the beginning of the study, and see how many of them you have been able to achieve.

Are there other things you have achieved that were not on your original list?

Spend some moments in prayer and make a commitment to continue with a regular and consistent prayer life.

A Personal Responsibility

Key Truth

" ... 'Do not be afraid. I bring you _____
_____ .

Today in the town of David a Saviour has been born to you;
_____ .' " Luke 2:10b–11

The world is anxiously waiting for good news. Scientists, philosophers, politicians and world leaders continually fail to produce any. The only hope for this planet is to hear the good news of the Gospel from the lips of those who have experienced Christ's transforming power.

List some of the difficulties you have with sharing your faith	Possible solutions

SHARE WITH THE GROUP AND TOGETHER MAKE A COMPOSITE LIST OF GOALS TO PURSUE DURING THE SIX WEEK STUDY.

GOALS _____

_____

_____

_____

The Great Commission

Next to worship the bold proclamation of our faith is the highest priority of the Christian Church.

"He said to them, ' _____
_____ *.' "* Mark 16:15

Definitions of "evangelism":

Meeting people where they are

Giving bread to the hungry

A farmer sowing the seed

Write out your own definition _____
_____

CONSIDER WHEN WAS THE LAST TIME YOU SHARED YOUR FAITH WITH SOMEONE?

Why Should We Evangelise?

☐ We have the only true message.   Add others to the list:

☐ Christ commanded it.   ☐ _____

☐ The world is going to hell.   ☐ _____

☐ That is why we were saved.   ☐ _____

☐ It is the job of the church.   ☐ _____

Number these reasons in your own order of priority.

COMPARE THE DIFFERENT CONCLUSIONS OF THE GROUP MEMBERS.

Word Study

GOSPEL: Euangelion – εὐαγγέλιον (Greek)
Originally a reward for good news, later becoming the Good News itself. A word used to describe the basic facts of the death, burial and resurrection of Christ.

Barriers to Overcome

If the New Testament places so much emphasis on the need for personal evangelism, why are so many Christians not engaged in it?

"I pray that faith ..." Philemon 6a

Where applicable, list how these affect your personal evangelism:

No Personal Salvation Experience
What has God promised about sin?
1 John 1:9

What two things do we need to do?
Romans 10:9

Indifference
Why was Paul such a firebrand?
Acts 9:1–9

What was the problem with the churches in Ephesus and Laodicea?
Revelation 2:4; 3:16

Lack of Biblical Knowledge
What was Paul's advice to Timothy? *2 Timothy 2:15*

What can all of us who know Christ do? *1 Peter 3:15*

Lack of Personality
What kind of people does God use? *1 Corinthians 1:26–31*

What is promised in times of timidity? *2 Corinthians 12:10*

Personal Problems
What sort of problems did Paul face? *2 Corinthians 11:23–28*

Did it prevent him sharing his faith? *1 Corinthians 9:16–18*

Fear of Rejection
What did Moses fear? *Exodus 4:1*

What is God's promise? *Isaiah 51:7–8*

Discouragement at No Response ▶
What is a key element of
Christian character?
1 Corinthians 4:2

_____

_____

_____

**DISCUSS WHAT IS THE
DIFFERENCE BETWEEN A
RESPONSIBILITY AND
RESPONSE?**

A Hard Heart ▶
What gripped the apostle Paul?
2 Corinthians 5:14

_____

What does God promise when we
come openly to Him?
Ezekiel 11:19

_____

_____

Excuses ▶
What is the difference
between reasons and excuses?
Luke 14:18–20

_____

What was Jeremiah's excuse?
Jeremiah 1:6–8

_____

 Practical Tip
Obstacles are there to be climbed over. Do not
see them as a threat but as a challenge. Climb
them one at a time.

 Word Study
CONSTRAIN: Sunechō – συνέχω (Greek)
To be seized totally, to be monopolised, to be
taken over by, to be consumed by.

Action Plan

During the next week share your personal experience of
Christ with at least two other Christians. It's good practice
for when you speak to non-Christians.

Recap

Christ has called each of us to share the good news of the
Gospel. Barriers and obstacles seek to prevent us, but each
one can be overcome with God's help.

A Heart for Evangelism

Key Truth

"O Jerusalem, Jerusalem, you who kill the prophets and stone those sent to you, _____

_____ but you were not willing." Matthew 23:37

When we comb the record of our Lord's life on this earth we find that there was never anyone with a heart so large as His. As He moved across ancient Palestine He had time and concern for all He met, whether like Peter they smelt of fish and the sea or like the woman of Samaria they bore the name of a harlot. He had room in His heart for them all.

EXPLORE SHARE WITH EACH OTHER HOW YOU GOT ON WITH YOUR ACTION PLAN AND HOW YOU FELT ABOUT SHARING YOUR PERSONAL EXPERIENCE OF CHRIST. WERE THERE ANY BARRIERS YOU FOUND HARD TO OVERCOME?

An Expanded Heart

How does God go about the task of expanding a Christian's heart? No one can be successful in evangelism until their own heart has been made large enough to take in others.

"*I run in the path of your commands, _____*

_____ ." Psalm 119:32

A Love for all Humanity

■ What is the challenge that confronts us? *Matthew 22:39*

■ What is the new commandment? *John 15:13*

EXPLAIN AND AMPLIFY WHAT JESUS' WORDS MEAN.

Moved with Compassion

■ How did Jesus demonstrate compassion? *Matthew 9:36–38; 20:34; Mark 1:41; Luke 7:13*

■ How did Jesus illustrate compassion? *Luke 10:25–37*

■ How did He view the people? *Mark 6:34*

Word Study

COMPASSION:
Splanchnizomai – σπλαγχνίζομαι **(Greek)**
To feel deeply, to yearn, to be inwardly gripped in the centre of your being.

RE-ENACT TAKE THE STORY OF THE GOOD SAMARITAN AND CHANGE THE CHARACTERS AND SETTING TO THE MODERN DAY. TWO OR THREE MEMBERS OF THE GROUP RETELL THE STORY.

■ List five major things that grip and motivate your life.

_____

_____

_____

_____

An Enlarged Vision

Many of us live our lives in compartments and maintain a narrow focus. If you and I do not spread the Gospel, the task will not get done.

"_____ , *the people perish:*

_____ ."

Proverbs 29:18 (AV)

Gospel Messengers

■ What has God called us to be? *2 Corinthians 5:20*

■ What is the implementation of this? *Mark 16:15–16*

Empowered from on High

■ What happens when the Holy Spirit comes upon us? *Acts 1:8*

■ What is the ministry of the Holy Spirit in evangelism? *John 16:8–11*

■ What was Paul able to say? *1 Corinthians 2:4*

■ List five ways to enlarge your evangelistic vision.

_____

_____

_____

_____

_____

An Enriched Church

The result of evangelism in the wider community is expansion and church growth.

"… praising God and enjoying the favour of all the people.

_____

_____ *."* Acts 2:47

■ What six lessons can we learn from Philip? *Acts 8:26–39*

_____

_____

_____

_____

_____

_____

 Word Study

CHURCH: Ekklesia – ἐκκλησία (Greek)
To call out; term for congregation. It denotes the New Testament congregation of the redeemed in a three-fold aspect: to be called out by Christ, to be called out to Christ and to be called out for Christ's purposes.

■ What is a key to building the Church? *Acts 19:8–10*

TALK THROUGH COME UP WITH TEN RELEVANT AND DIFFERENT WAYS YOU COULD EVANGELISE YOUR COMMUNITY.

PAUSE FOR PRAYER SPEND SOME MOMENTS IN PRAYER ASKING GOD TO GIVE AN EXPANDED HEART, ENLARGED VISION AND AN ENRICHED CHURCH.

Action Plan

Stand on your local high street for at least half an hour and watch people. Think of heaven, think of hell, then watch the people again. Ask God to help you see them as He does, lost sheep without a shepherd. Allow Christ's sense of compassion to touch you.

Recap

So often our hearts become hard to the lost. God wants to give us a love and compassion for humanity to move us from our narrow focus to reach out to others, so that their lives can be changed by Christ and enriched within the Church.

The Master Soul Winner

Key Truth

"The fruit of the righteous is a tree of life, _____

_____ ."

Proverbs 11:30

The message of salvation and forgiveness is the central theme of the Gospels. They trace the steps of the master soul winner at work redeeming the lost and reconciling a sinful world to a holy God.

SHARE HOW YOU GOT ON WITH YOUR ACTION PLAN. WHAT DID YOU FEEL DURING AND AFTER IT?

Sharing the Truth

Truth is the only thing that will bring about true and lasting change in human nature.

" 'Then you will know the truth, _____

_____ .' " John 8:32

v6 ◀ Verses from John 4 (The Woman at the Well) that relate to this step in soul winning.

v10

■ What did Jesus declare? *John 14:6*

v13–14

v18 ■ Why is it necessary to expose people to the truth? *John 8:43–45*

v21–24

List some of the lies that are projected at people

v26 through television:

Examples: God is irrelevant

Cheating is acceptable

_____

_____

Seizing the Opportunity

Often evangelistic opportunities present themselves and, if not taken, are soon gone.

"As long as it is day, we must do the work of him who sent me.
_____ *."* John 9:4

 v7

■ When are we wise? *Ephesians 5:15–16; Colossians 4:5*

■ What did Jesus exhort? *John 4:35*

TALK THROUGH SOME OF THE OPPORTUNITIES THAT PRESENT THEMSELVES TO YOU DURING YOUR WEEK.

 ## Word Study

OPPORTUNITY: Kairos – καιρός (Greek)
A particular time that affords a special possibility or moment. The necessity to grasp it while it is there, as it is not guaranteed to come again.

Tuning in to the Felt Need

Sensitivity to the immediate concerns of a person shows a caring attitude and a genuine interest.

" _____
_____
but we have one who has been tempted in every way, just as we are – yet was without sin."* Hebrews 4:15

v7

■ What was Paul's philosophy? *1 Corinthians 9:19–23*

■ How can we reach out to the troubled? *2 Corinthians 1:3–5*

■ What needs to be evident to all? *Philippians 4:5*

List some ways we can show insensitivity:
Examples: Imposing our views
Lack of concern
_____
_____

Practical Tip

Always start the conversation with what is familiar to the person, before you move on to share things they are unfamiliar with — remember Jesus started with the water.

Overcoming Obstacles

Often people put up resistance because they do not understand the depth of their own need.

"But they all alike _____ ." Luke 14:18a

v9
v12
v19

■ How did Paul deal with the philosophers? *Acts 17:16–32*

■ What underlies every human condition? *Isaiah 55:1–3*

■ What objection did Felix make? *Acts 24:25*

Show Respect for the Person

We need to accept the person as they are. Although we do not condone sin we do not condemn the person.

" 'The Son of Man came eating and drinking, and they say, "Here is a glutton and a drunkard, _____ ." But wisdom is proved right by her actions.' "* Matthew 11:19

v16

■ How did Jesus approach the Emmaus road disciples? *Luke 24:13–27*

■ What does Jesus not do? *John 3:17*

■ How are we to share our faith? *1 Peter 3:15*

Gently but Firmly Face the Issue of Sin

Sin is universal and a person needs to come to the realisation of their own personal sin and guilt.

"All of us have become like one who is unclean, _____ ; we all shrivel up like a leaf, and like the wind our sins sweep us away." Isaiah 64:6

v17–18

■ How did Jesus deal with the woman? *John 8:1–11*

v17–18 ■ How are we deceived? *1 John 1:8; Psalm 53:3*

■ What is a sure fact? *Numbers 32:23*

TALK ABOUT **WHAT IS THE DIFFERENCE BETWEEN SIN AND SINS (OF THE FLESH)? ISAIAH 14:13–14**

Word Study

SIN: Hamartia – ἁμαρτία (Greek)
Missing the true goal and scope of life, missing the mark; giving offence in relation to God with emphasis on the resulting guilt.

Reveal the Saviour

Sin cannot be forgotten or covered; it can only be forgiven by the risen Saviour.

"He himself bore our sins in his body on the tree, —————————————————————; by his wounds you have been healed." 1 Peter 2:24

v26 ■ How did Paul reveal Christ? *Galatians 2:20*

v29 ■ How did Paul describe the Corinthians? *2 Corinthians 3:2–3*

Action Plan

This week be alert for an opportunity to follow the example of the master soul winner. Prayerfully seek out someone who does not know Him and follow His pattern of sharing with them.

Recap

We need to recognise and take advantage of evangelistic opportunities when they present themselves, showing respect for the person and tuning in to their felt need. Although they will present obstacles we can share the truth, gently but firmly facing the issue of sin and the saving grace of Jesus.

Lifestyle Evangelism

Key Truth

"Live such good lives among the pagans that, though they accuse you of doing wrong, _____

_____ on the day he visits us."

I Peter 2:12

Some Christians see evangelism as something that is done at a particular time on special occasions. But evangelism should not just be kept for Sundays and special events. It should permeate our daily actions and activities.

Christlike Qualities

Jesus not only gave us the Sermon on the Mount, but exemplified it by His life. He not only laid down the principles for life, but lived them out perfectly.

■ List the characteristics Christ outlined. *Matthew 5:1–11*

Right attitude	Wrong attitude
1.	1.
2.	2.
3.	3.
4.	4.
5.	5.
6.	6.
7.	7.
8.	8.

Dr Billy Graham calls the beatitudes the beautiful attitudes. List them with their meaning, and also list the opposite attitude.

■ What are we like when the beatitudes are displayed through us? *Matthew 5:12–16*

FOR THOUGHT IF YOU WERE PROSECUTED FOR BEING A CHRISTIAN, WOULD THERE BE ENOUGH EVIDENCE TO CONVICT YOU?

 Word Study

BLESSED: Makarios – μακάριος (Greek)
To be fully satisfied. A person whom God makes fully satisfied, not because of favourable circumstances, but because He indwells the believer through Christ.

Indwelling Christ

Christ not only brings salvation but comes to live His life through us.

"To them God has chosen to make known among the Gentiles the glorious riches of this mystery, which is _____ _____ ."
Colossians 1:27

■ What was Paul's prayer for the Ephesians? *Ephesians 3:16–19*

■ What is essential for knowing the indwelling Christ? *1 John 3:24*

■ What do we become partakers of? *2 Peter 1:3–4*

A Conversational Approach

People do not relate well to pious or religious language. We need to talk naturally in everyday words that can be understood.

" _____ those he redeemed from the hand of the foe ..."
Psalm 107:2

■ What was Paul's approach? *1 Corinthians 2:1–10*

■ Rewrite Romans 3:21–25 in a few sentences of your own words, then share with the group.

Practical Tip

Always listen to the vocabulary level of the other person and avoid jargon words and spiritual clichés.

Sowing Seeds

The principle in Scripture is that one sows, one waters and another reaps, but remember sowing always comes first.

"Remember this: Whoever sows sparingly will also reap sparingly, _____ _____ ." 2 Corinthians 9:6

■ What is the principle of sowing? *Matthew 13:3–9*

■ Think through at least ten different ways you could sow the seed of the gospel.

Setting an Example

A lot of non-believers feel that all church-goers are hypocrites. We have a responsibility to prove them wrong.

"_____ _____ might ..." Ecclesiastes 9:10a

■ Work out five ways of setting an example from *1 Peter 2:9–21.*

■ What did Paul admonish the Ephesians for? *Ephesians 4:28*

Take Time to Listen

Most of us are better talkers than we are listeners because we prefer to hear the sound of our own voices.

"My dear brothers, take note of this: _____ _____ , slow to speak and slow to become angry ..." James 1:19

■ What is our tendency? *Proverbs 18:13*

■ What phrase appears seven times in these chapters? *Revelation 2–3*

Practical Tip

We have two ears and one mouth – learn to listen twice as much as you talk!

EXERCISE BREAK INTO PAIRS. ONE OF THE PAIR SHARES SOMETHING FOR TWO MINUTES, THE OTHER LISTENS. AFTER TWO MINUTES THE LISTENER REPEATS IT BACK IN 30 SECONDS. THEN REVERSE THE EXERCISE. THE LEADER TIMES IT.

Make a Definite Impression

We impress people more by who we are, than what we say.

"*Much* _____ .
Therefore stand in awe of God." Ecclesiastes 5:7

■ What was Paul's instruction? *Colossians 4:5–6*

■ How are we to live? *1 Peter 2:12*

List some of the ways we can make an impact on people.

Examples: Being consistent
Manner of conversation
_____
_____
_____

Action Plan

Take some of the ideas you have for sowing some gospel seeds, and sow some this week.

Recap

As we allow Christ to indwell us more deeply His attitudes and characteristics will be seen in our actions and words. By our daily conversation, our willingness to listen and the example we set, we can be sure Christ in us will make His impression through us.

The Practice of Evangelism

Key Truth

"These twelve Jesus sent out with the following instructions: 'Do not go among the Gentiles or enter any town of the Samaritans.

_____

_____

_____ ." ' " Matthew 10:5–7

We can never expect to change the world by focusing merely on the theory of evangelism. What we have learned must be put into practice, on a regular basis. Review last week's action plan.

Pray Daily for the Unconverted

People are often resistant to the Gospel, but prayer is the bridge we can build to gain access into their heart.

"... _For he bore the sin of many, and_ _____

_____ ." Isaiah 53:12b

■ Draw up a list of non-Christians to pray for.

_____   _____

_____   _____

_____   _____

_____   _____

■ What did Paul exhort Timothy to do? _1 Timothy 2:1–4_

■ What is God's greatest desire? _2 Peter 3:9_

■ What pattern did the psalmist have? _Psalm 88:9_

Word Study

SALVATION: Sōtēria – σωτηρία **(Greek)**
Deliverance from danger to safety; preservation from great harm.

Share Your Testimony

You may not be a great orator, but you can share your own life experience in your own words.

"So _____

_____ *Lord* ..." 2 Timothy 1:8a

■ What four elements are essential to a testimony?

To Do JOT DOWN IN ABOUT 100 WORDS THESE FOUR ELEMENTS OF YOUR OWN PERSONAL STORY.

SHARE BREAK DOWN INTO PAIRS. EACH MEMBER OF THE GROUP SHARE YOUR TESTIMONY WITH THE OTHER PERSON IN THREE MINUTES.

■ What did Peter and John say? *Acts 4:20*

■ What must we always be prepared to do? *1 Peter 3:15*

Share the Scriptural Basis

Each of us can take time to learn and memorise a basic Biblical framework.

" '*In the past God overlooked such ignorance, but now he commands* _____

_____ .' " Acts 17:30

Learn the ABC of salvation:

A _____ *Romans 3:23; 1 Timothy 1:15*

B _____ *John 3:16; Acts 2:21*

C _____ *1 John 1:8–9; Romans 10:9*

(See answer 1 at the foot of the next page)

Word Study

REPENTANCE – Metanoeō – μετανοέω (Greek)
A complete change of mind and attitude; to turn completely around; always signifying a change for the better; a radical transformation by a deliberate action.

Point to the Uniqueness of Christ

People often say "I believe in God". You can respond by saying "Which God? I believe in the God and Father of our Lord Jesus Christ."

" _____ , *and through him to reconcile to himself all things, whether things on earth or things in heaven, by making peace through his blood, shed on the cross."* Colossians 1:19–20

Fill in three unique characteristics of Jesus:

S

_____ *Matthew 16:16*

_____ *1 Peter 3:18*

_____ *Acts 5:30–31*

(See answer 2 at the foot of the page)

Commitment to Christ

People often want to relate to Christ on their terms, but only an obedient commitment to His Lordship brings salvation.

" ' _____ , ' *Jesus said, 'and I will make you fishers of men.' "* Matthew 4:19

■ Why do people struggle with commitment? *Luke 9:57–62*

■ What does the cross represent? *John 12:24–26; Matthew 10:38*

■ What does to deny ourselves mean? *Matthew 16:24–26*

Answers: 1. Acknowledge; Believe; Confess 2. Son of God; Substitute for Sin; Saviour who is risen.

Confession of Faith

Encourage a new convert to share their faith with someone else.

"... and every tongue _____ _____ , to the glory of God the Father."
Philippians 2:11

■ What two things should we encourage a person to do? *Romans 10:9–10*

■ What did Jesus declare? *Luke 12:8–9*

 Practical Tip
It is helpful for someone to share their new found faith with another believer first.

Action Plan

This week, learn and memorise the Scriptural basics of the plan of salvation and share them with another believer so that you are confident you have grasped them.

Recap

Pray daily for the unconverted and be willing to share your testimony and a Scriptural framework for your faith and experience. Focus upon Christ and His saving grace and encourage a commitment to Him followed by a confession of faith.

Evangelism Perpetuated

Key Truth

"God blessed them and said to them, '_____
_____ number ...' "

Genesis 1:28a

Evangelism is not merely an occupation but an outcome. It is not something imposed but something inherent. We cancel the power of the Gospel in ourselves unless we pass on its power to others.

Fruitfulness

Fruitfulness is the natural outgrowth of the life contained in the tree.

"So, my brothers, you also died to the law through the body of Christ ... in order _____
_____ ." Romans 7:4

■ What did Jesus teach on fruitfulness? *John 15:1–8*

■ What was Paul's prayer? *Colossians 1:10*

DISCUSS THE RELATIONSHIP BETWEEN GOOD WORKS AND EVANGELISM.

Empowered Witness

When a witness is called to court he is there to declare the truth as he has come to know it and understand it. Once completed it is the advocate who

"But you will receive my power when the Holy Spirit comes on you; _____
..., and to the ends of the earth." Acts 1:8

■ What did Jesus promise? *Luke 24:45–49*

■ How did the early disciples view themselves? *Acts 10:39–43*

■ What is the key work of the Holy Spirit? *John 16:8–11*

presses the truth home for conviction.

Word Study

CONVICTION: Elenchō – ἐλέγχω **(Greek)**
To show one is in the wrong and to put to -shame; to convince of error and wrong doing; to detect and strongly face someone with the hidden things of the heart.

Creative Activity

What greater creative activity can there be than to bring spiritual sons and daughters to birth – creating for eternity.

"In reply Jesus declared, 'I tell you the truth, no-one can see the kingdom of God _____ .' "
John 3:3

■ What will overcome the world? *1 John 5:1–5*

■ Who is the "spiritual midwife"? *John 3:7–8*

■ What sort of creative seed are we sowing? *1 Peter 1:23*

 Practical Tip
Remember that one sows, one waters, and another reaps. Rarely do all three things happen at once. Do not force the birth process.

THOUGHT BIG OAKS FROM LITTLE ACORNS GROW.

The Contagious Life

As the joy of the Lord and His grace buoy us up, our lives will overflow to others.

" 'Heal the sick, raise the dead, cleanse those who have leprosy, drive out demons. _____ .' "
Matthew 10:8

■ What is the principle of receiving? *Luke 6:38; Acts 20:35*

■ How are we like artesian wells? *Isaiah 12:2–3*

■ What did Jesus promise? *John 7:38*

ASK YOURSELF IF MY FAITH WERE CHICKEN POX – HOW MANY OTHER PEOPLE WOULD NOW HAVE IT?

The Compelling Choice

When Christ's heartbeat grips us deeply there is a passion to share with others.

"Woe to you who are _____ _____ on Mount Samaria ..." Amos 6:1a

■ How did Paul feel about evangelism? *1 Corinthians 9:16*

■ What was Paul's ambition? *Romans 15:20*

■ How did the man respond? *Luke 8:39*

PAUSE FOR PRAYER STOP FOR A FEW MOMENTS AND ASK GOD TO KINDLE A BURNING PASSION IN YOUR SOUL.

The Universal Thirst

At the core of everyone's being there is a deep longing and thirst for truth and reality.

"_____, for the living God. When can I go and meet with God?" Psalm 42:2

■ What is the result of finding the living water? *Isaiah 12:2–3*

■ What did Jesus unconditionally promise? *John 4:14*

ACTIVITY ASK YOURSELF – WHAT DO I LONG FOR? NARROW IT DOWN TO TWO OR THREE THINGS – BE HONEST WITH YOUR ANSWERS. SHARE WITH THE GROUP AND EXPLORE TOGETHER HOW THE HEART'S DEEP LONGINGS CAN BE MET.

The Pure Motive

Our motivation for sharing the Gospel should not be out of duty or to be applauded by others, but out of our love for the Saviour.

"_____, because we are convinced that one died for all, and therefore all died." 2 Corinthians 5:14

■ What did Jesus hold against the church at Ephesus? *Revelation 2:4*

■ What did Jesus predict? *Matthew 24:12*

■ What antidote did Jesus give? *Revelation 2:5*

Read John 20:21 List down some of the elements of the Father's will that Christ fulfilled in relation to evangelism and what that means for you.

AS ≠	SO
The Father has sent me	**I am sending you**
Examples:	
Christ comes as a servant.	**I will go out as a servant.**
Christ showed compassion.	**I will go out with compassion.**
Christ did not condemn.	**I will not condemn.**

Action Plan

Arrange a group evangelistic activity implementing the things you have learned over these last six weeks.

Recap

When my life is on fire for Jesus, empowered by the Holy Spirit to witness, I will bear fruit by creatively winning men and women to Jesus. This is a choice I gladly make, compelled by my love for Jesus – who alone can meet the universal thirst of every human heart.

Final Thoughts

What are the five most significant things about sharing your faith that you have learned over the last six weeks? Take a few moments in prayer to commit yourself to regularly and naturally sharing your faith with those who do not know Christ.

Created for Praise

 Key Truth

"

_____

for his unfailing love and his wonderful deeds for men ... "
Psalm 107:8

A Christian who knows how to fill his life with praise faces life buoyantly and confidently because in every situation, no matter how dark and difficult, he is conscious of God's mercy and grace streaming from heaven.

Why do you think praise is important?	List any problems you have with the concept of praise

SHARE WITH THE GROUP AND MAKE A LIST OF GOALS TO PURSUE DURING THIS STUDY:

_____

_____

Practical Tip
After setting overall goals it is important to establish the immediate goal, i.e. what is the next step to take.

Write out your own definition of praise:

_____

_____

Praise the Creator

There are two types of Christians, those who take life for granted and those who take it with gratitude and praise.

"Let everything that has breath _____

_____ *."* Psalm 150:6

> **List, from Psalm 145, some of the reasons why we praise our Creator**

■ What was the psalmist's response and exhortation?

At All Times

There can be no doubt to even the most casual reader of Scripture that praise is a significant element of our daily walk with God.

"I will extol the Lord _____

_____ *on my lips."* Psalm 34:1

■ What are we to do continually? *Hebrews 13:15*

■ What does a sacrifice of praise mean? *Hebrews 13:15*

THINK WHAT ARE THE TIMES WHEN YOU FIND IT MOST DIFFICULT TO PRAISE THE LORD? SHARE THESE WITH THE GROUP.

Expression Deepens Impression

C. S. Lewis said we delight to praise the things we enjoy because the praise not merely expresses the pleasure we feel but completes it.

" _____

– those he redeemed from the hand of the foe ..." Psalm 107:2

■ What did Jesus encourage the man to do? *Mark 5:19–20*

■ What are we to do when we come together? *Ephesians 5:19–20*

Practical Tip

It is good to express our thoughts to others. As we do, we see them with greater clarity and they are more deeply impressed into our own minds and spirits.

Word Study

WORSHIP:
Proskuneō – προσκυνέω (Greek)
To ascribe adoration to God for who He is. To give Him reverence and homage.
Sebomai – σεβομαι (Greek)
To revere and honour, stressing the characteristic of awe and feelings of deep devotion.

God Inhabits our Praises

As we give our praises to God as an expression of our love and gratitude, God comes and dwells amongst us.

" _____

you are the praise of Israel." Psalm 22:3

■ What did Jesus say? *Luke 6:38*

■ What did the psalmist declare? *Psalm 30*

PAUSE FOR PRAISE STOP AND SPEND A FEW MINUTES GIVING PRAISE TO GOD FOR HIS GOODNESS.

The Root of Sin

Thanklessness and ingratitude is the outward expression of self-centredness which lies at the heart of all sin.

"*Instead, you have set yourself up against the Lord of heaven … You praised the gods of silver and gold, of bronze, iron, wood and stone, which cannot see or hear or understand. _____

_____

_____.*" Daniel 5:23

■ Look at *Genesis 3* and *Romans 1:18–23*.
What is the relationship between unthankfulness and sin?

DISCUSS YOUR CONCLUSIONS IN THE GROUP.

Healthy Praise

Whilst praise is not a guarantee of health, when we fail to praise our spirits are impoverished.

"_____

and make music to your name, O Most High ..." Psalm 92:1

■ What was the psalmist's perspective? _Psalm 139:13–14_

■ What had the nine lepers missed? _Luke 17:11–19_

■ What is one of the things we are to think on?
Philippians 4:8

SING TOGETHER THE CHORUS "GIVE THANKS WITH A GRATEFUL HEART".

Loaded with Benefits

Mercies can be found at the heart of life's circumstances and we can see something to be grateful for in the most dark and dismal situations.

"_Praise the Lord, O my soul, and_ _____

_____ ..._" Psalm 103:2

■ What happened when Paul and Silas sang in prison?
Acts 16:25–32

■ What are some of the benefits of the man who delights in the Lord? _Psalm 112_

COUNT YOUR BLESSINGS GO ROUND THE GROUP ONE AFTER THE OTHER AND IN ONE SENTENCE EXPRESS A BLESSING YOU ENJOY – DO THIS SEVERAL TIMES.

Action Plan

At the end of each day this week, spend a few moments reviewing the day and focus on five things to give God thanks for before you go to sleep.

Recap

Praise is focused upon our Lord and Creator for His goodness. It is an outward expression of our inner trust. Thanklessness and ingratitude are sin and even in difficult times there is much to praise God for. When we do not praise Him our spirits are impoverished, but when we do we feel the closeness of His presence.

The Power of Praise

🔑 Key Truth

"... and provide for those who grieve in Zion – to bestow on them a crown of beauty instead of ashes, _____

_____.

They will be called oaks of righteousness, a planting of the Lord for the display of his splendour." Isaiah 61:3

The Scriptures record instances when in difficult circumstances praise was offered to God. The result was that God worked a miracle that defied human logic.

SHARE WITH THE GROUP HOW YOU GOT ON WITH YOUR ACTION PLAN. DID IT MAKE ANY DIFFERENCE TO YOUR SLEEP?

The Sacrifice of Praise

Praise in difficult circumstances needs to be expressed in faith. Praise is an expression of trust in God despite the circumstance.

"Through Jesus, therefore, let us continually offer to God

_____

_____ *."* Hebrews 13:15

■ What are we to be? *Hebrews 13:5*

■ What is the will of God? *1 Thessalonians 5:18*

■ What was Paul's instruction to the Ephesians? *Ephesians 5:20*

DISCUSS THE RELATIONSHIP BETWEEN CONTENTMENT AND PRAISE.

Victory through Praise

When we realise our own powerlessness, put trust in God and praise Him for His abundant power, we are then able to see that power at work.

"_____ _____ against the men of Ammon and Moab and Mount Seir who were invading Judah, and they were defeated._" 2 Chronicles 20:22

■ Read verses 14–24 of _2 Chronicles 20._

■ What perspective enabled them to be an army of singers? _Verse 15_

■ What conviction did this produce? _Verse 17_

■ What response did this bring? _Verses 18–19_

THINK CAN YOU THINK OF ANY OTHER BIBLICAL ACCOUNTS WHERE VICTORY WAS RELATED TO PRAISE? LOOK THEM UP AND READ THEM.

The Fall of Jericho

When confronted by insurmountable walls that threaten to overwhelm, the shout of praise confirms our trust in God.

"_When you hear them sound a long blast on the trumpets, _____ ; then the wall of the city will collapse and the people will go up, every man straight in._" Joshua 6:5

■ What was the result of the psalmist's praise? _Psalm 138:1–3_

■ What can we be sure of when we trust and delight ourselves in the Lord? _Psalm 37:3–6_

SELECT A VICTORY PRAISE SONG AND SING IT TOGETHER.

The Way of Deliverance

Whatever your problem, turn from it in trust and praise God, magnify the Lord. The God who lived in David's day is just the same today.

*"I call to the Lord, who is worthy of praise, _____
_____ ."* 2 Samuel 22:4

■ How did David mingle prayer and praise? *Psalm 144*

■ What was Paul's testimony? *2 Timothy 4:16–18*

List some of the areas of praise and link them to prayer. For example:

Praise	Prayer
Thank You, Lord, that You are the great provider.	I come to You and place my financial needs before You.
Thank You, Lord, for You are the One that heals.	I come to You and place my physical needs before You.

Thanks Precede a Miracle

After Jesus gave thanks, ordinary bread became miracle bread; fish sandwiches fed five thousand men besides women and children.

*"Taking the five loaves and the two fish and looking up to heaven, _____ .
... They all ate and were satisfied ..."* Matthew 14:19b, 20a

■ What view did Jesus have of praise? *Luke 19:37–40*

■ What did Jesus do before His darkest moment? *Luke 22:17–19*

 ## Word Study

MIRACLE: Dunamis – δύναμις (Greek)
Works of supernatural origin and character such as cannot be produced by natural means or agents; events that defy natural laws.

Singing Jailbirds

Despite their circumstances when serving God, Paul and Silas praised instead of complaining. It became the note around which God constructed a symphony of sound that broke through all natural barriers.

"About midnight Paul and Silas were praying _____
_____ *, and the other prisoners were listening to them."* Acts 16:25

■ Why can we give glory to God?
Ephesians 3:20–21; Philippians 4:19–20

■ How should we serve? *1 Peter 4:11*

PAUSE FOR PRAISE SPEND A FEW MINUTES EXPRESSING PRAISES TO GOD.

Practical Tip
Remember we praise God for who He is, not what He does. When we focus our praise on Him, the problems are put in their proper perspective.

Try Praise

Praise is as powerful as prayer in bringing out spiritual victories. Mingle the two together.

"When I am afraid, I will trust in you. _____
_____ *;*
I will not be afraid. What can mortal man do to me?"
Psalm 56:3–4

■ What are some of the things the psalmist praises the Lord for? *Psalm 146*

■ What did the psalmist say he would do? *Psalm 34:1*

Action Plan

This week write your own psalm of praise, ready to share with the group next week.

Recap

As we offer praise in the face of battles and struggles there is great power. As a result, victory and deliverance follow and miracles happen.

Characteristics of a True Worshipper

> **Key Truth**
>
> " 'God is spirit, and his worshippers _____
> _____ .' " John 4:24

We have been seeing the fact that praise releases God's power into certain situations and that heart-felt praise is often a prelude to a miracle. However, we need to keep this in balance with the fact that God's Word spells out a number of conditions and requirements for a thankful worshipper.

DISCUSS YOUR ACTION PLAN. READ OUT YOUR PSALMS TO EACH OTHER.

An Obedient Heart

God considers obedience to His Word to be more important than extravagant sacrifice. What we sing or say should reflect the commitment of our hearts.

"But Samuel replied: 'Does the Lord delight in burnt offerings and sacrifices as much as in obeying the voice of the Lord?

_____ ,

and to heed is better than the fat of rams.' " 1 Samuel 15:22

■ Why is it easy for the obedient heart to praise?
James 1:22–25

Explain each of the following in a few words:
PRAISE –
WORSHIP –
LORDSHIP –
OBEDIENCE –

Heartfelt Praise

The only sound that reaches up to heaven is heartfelt praise.

"Away with the noise of your songs! _____ _____ ." Amos 5:23

■ What did the psalmist confirm? *Psalm 138:1–2*

■ What complaint did the Lord have? *Isaiah 29:13*

■ What was Paul's exhortation? *Colossians 3:23*

Broken Relationships

A thankful worshipper is one who takes time to restore and maintain good relationships with fellow worshippers.

"… leave your gift there in front of the altar. _____ _____ ; then come and offer your gift." Matthew 5:24

■ What is the first step to reconciliation?
Mark 11:25; Luke 17:4

■ What is the next step to reconciliation that we should take? *Matthew 18:15*

■ What is the basis of forgiving others?
Ephesians 4:32; Colossians 3:13

 # Word Study

FORGIVE:
Aphiēmi – ἀφίημι (Greek)
To completely cancel; to free someone from the deserved penalty; to unconditionally release someone from the offence committed; to restore a relationship to the same as it was prior to the offence.

Humility

One of the greatest dangers we face as we grow in our Christian life is spiritual pride. A humble mind is the soil out of which thanksgiving naturally grows.

"The sacrifices of God are a broken spirit; a broken _____ _____ , O God, you will not despise." Psalm 51:17

■ Why were the Pharisee's thanks misplaced? *Luke 18:11*

■ What does the Lord require? *Micah 6:8*

 Practical Tip

Humility is not self-denegration, or self-belittlement. It is knowing who we are in Christ yet choosing to esteem others.

THINK THROUGH SOME WAYS IN WHICH HUMILITY CAN BE DISPLAYED.

A Rejoicing Spirit

Praise that is not given cheerfully but grudgingly falls far short of God's ideal.

"... _____ , I will be joyful in God my Saviour." *Habakkuk 3:18*

■ What was Paul able to say? *2 Corinthians 6:10*

■ What was Mary's response? *Luke 1:47*

Divine Grace

Graciousness towards others means a willingness to show goodwill, be magnanimous and large hearted. You cannot praise God genuinely if you have a bitter spirit.

"Let the word of Christ dwell in you richly as you teach and admonish one another with all wisdom, and as you sing psalms, hymns and spiritual songs _____ _____ ." Colossians 3:16

■ What was Paul able to testify? *1 Timothy 1:14*

■ How did Paul encourage Timothy? *2 Timothy 2:1*

_____

_____

_____

Faith

As long as we love God and have faith to believe that everything that comes our way can be used by Him, then nothing can stop praise swelling in our hearts.

" _____ ,
because anyone who comes to him must believe that he exists and that he rewards those who earnestly seek him." Hebrews 11:6

■ What does faith enable us to do? *1 John 5:4–5*

■ What does faith focus on? *1 Corinthians 2:5*

■ Why did Paul delight in hardship and persecution? *2 Corinthians 12:9–10*

Action Plan

Think through during the week the area of your relationships to see if there are any that are broken or fractured. Follow the steps of reconciliation mentioned in this study.

Recap

The characteristics of a true worshipper are an obedient and passionate heart, accompanied by a rejoicing and gracious spirit. A true worshipper restores broken relationships and walks through this life with humility and faith.

Praise Him with your Whole Being

⚿ Key Truth

"Praise the Lord. _____
_____ in the council of the upright and in the assembly."
Psalm 111:1

When we come to worship it is important that we understand something of the wonderful design God has placed within our being. Praise involves the whole of our personality: our feelings, our thoughts and our wills.

SHARE HOW YOU GOT ON WITH YOUR ACTION PLAN.

Working with God's Design

God has not only designed us with a personality, but a spirit and body too. These also have an important part to play in our worship.

"*Praise the Lord, O my soul;* _____
_____ ." Psalm 103:1

■ What produces life? *Romans 8:6*

■ What three dimensions must praise also relate to?
1 Thessalonians 5:23

■ What did the psalmist address? *Psalm 42:5*

List ways of praising God in three dimensions:

Spirit	Soul	Body

Think

Allow your mind to ponder on the blessings and goodness of God and be thankful.

"Finally, brothers, whatever is true, whatever is noble, whatever is right, whatever is pure, whatever is lovely, whatever is admirable — _____

_____ — think about such things." Philippians 4:8

■ Where does renewal take place? *Ephesians 4:23*

■ What was the psalmist's prayer? *Psalm 19:14*

■ What did the psalmist rejoice in? *Psalm 119:11–16*

QUOTE A MAN IS NOT WHAT HE THINKS HE IS, BUT WHAT HE THINKS, HE IS.

No Reason for Thanksgiving

In this God-denying, un-grateful and confused generation, let your voice be heard giving grateful thanks to God.

"All this is for your benefit, so that the grace that is reaching more and more people _____

_____." 2 Corinthians 4:15

■ What was the psalmist convinced of? *Psalm 136*

■ How did he confirm it to himself? *Psalm 136*

TO DO TAKE THE PATTERN OF THIS PSALM AND WRITE A PSALM FOR THE GROUP WITH EVERYONE PUTTING A VERSE IN.

E.g. I thank the Lord I am saved,
                          His love endures forever.

A Journal of Gratefulness

Confucius said that the faintest ink is stronger than the greatest memory. Why not record the goodness of God in a permanent form?

"I thank my God every time _____."
Philippians 1:3

■ What did the psalmist say he would do? *Psalm 79:13*

■ What are we to overflow with? *Colossians 2:7*

Thanksgiving for Everything

Make a practice of thanking people even if you have to go to a little trouble to locate them.

"... _____
for this is God's will for you in Christ Jesus."
1 Thessalonians 5:18

■ What happened to the man who delivered the city? *Ecclesiastes 9:13–16*

■ What is it easy to do? *Genesis 40:12–15, 20–23*

■ What did they fail in? *Judges 8:33–35*

List five people you can express thanks to:

Name	Reason to be thankful

■ Break down into twos and talk through your lists.

A Ransomed Sinner

It is so easy to take our Christian experience for granted, and the enormous price and sacrifice Christ paid to redeem us.

"_____ *for his indescribable gift!"*
2 Corinthians 9:15

List the spiritual blessings we have in Christ. Ephesians 1:3–14

SHARE TOGETHER WHAT THESE MEAN.

Achieving the Impossible

When we use our wills to do what God asks us to – praise Him, even though we do not feel like it – He responds to this act of faith by bringing about a change in our feelings.

"… _____ to will and to act according to his good purpose." Philippians 2:13

List the problems of Jeremiah. Lamentations 3:15–20	What did Jeremiah call to mind? Lamentations 3:21–26

What was the result?

Action Plan

This week commence your journal of gratefulness and at the end of each day make an entry. Contact the five people on your list and express your thanks to them.

Recap

As we work with God's design, praise affects every area of our being. As our minds dwell on God's goodness we have much reason to be grateful. It is helpful to record our gratefulness and to express it to those who have been good to us. It is so easy to take for granted the blessings of God. When we choose to give thanks despite the circumstances, our feelings feel the impact.

Reacting to Life Circumstances

Key Truth

"I am not saying this because I am in need, for I have learned to be content whatever the circumstances. I know what it is to be in need, and I know what it is to have plenty. _____

_____ ,
whether well fed or hungry, whether living in plenty or in want."
Philippians 4:11–12

There are various ways in which we can respond to life's difficulties and problems, but the Christian way is transformation. That is, facing life as it comes day by day and transforming the bad things to something positive and beneficial. If you adopt this attitude in life and make it a central conviction then inevitably you will become a praising person.

SHARE HOW YOU GOT ON WITH YOUR ACTION PLAN, AND HOW THE PEOPLE RESPONDED TO YOU.

A Central Truth

In the life of a Christian, it is not so much what happens to us that is important, but how we respond to what happens.

"_____ , *my brothers, whenever you face trials of many kinds ...*" James 1:2

■ What sort of circumstances did Paul have to endure? *2 Corinthians 11:23–31*

■ How did Paul respond to his difficult circumstances? *2 Corinthians 12:10*

■ How did Paul view life? *1 Timothy 6:6–8*

DISCUSS THE DIFFERENCE BETWEEN REACTING AND RESPONDING.

The Way of Transformation

God is at work turning every stumbling block into a stepping stone.

"... _____,
your right hand will hold me fast." Psalm 139:10

■ What does the renewing of the mind do? *Romans 12:2*

■ What was Paul able to say? *2 Corinthians 6:3–10;
Romans 5:2–5*

From 2 Corinthians 6:3–10 list on a separate sheet of paper ten difficult circumstances with ten positive responses.

 Word Study

TRANSFORM:
Metamorphoō – μεταμορφόω (Greek)
To change into another form; to undergo a complete change by the power of God, that will be seen in both character and conduct; change from natural to spiritual.

Making Everything Serve

When we are able to make the situations of life a servant to the purposes of God, our response to their transformation is one of praise.

*"We are hard pressed on every side,_____;
perplexed, _____ ; persecuted, _____
_____ , struck down, _____."*
2 Corinthians 4:8–9

■ How did Joseph view his setback? *Genesis 45:5–9*

■ How did Paul view his imprisonment?
Ephesians 6:20; Philippians 1:12–14

A Radiant Philosophy

We are what we respond to. A strength of Christ's life was His poised and peaceful response to all life situations.

*"Keep your lives free from the love of money and _____
_____ , because God has said,
'Never will I leave you; never will I forsake you.' "*
Hebrews 13:5

■ What was God's promise to Joshua? *Joshua 1:5*

- What was Paul's approach to life? *Romans 8:31–37*
- What was the attitude of the Hebrew boys? *Daniel 3:16–18*

DISCUSS THE STATEMENT – "WE ARE WHAT WE RESPOND TO". GIVE FIVE POSITIVE AND FIVE NEGATIVE EXAMPLES.

Practical Tip

God has promised to supply a corresponding source of grace for every life circumstance. Do not react spontaneously, but stop for a few moments prayer to draw on God's grace.

Redemptive Reaction

The actions of Jesus were wonderful but so were His reactions. His reactions were just as redemptive as His actions.

"But he said to me, '_____, for my power is made perfect in weakness.' Therefore I will boast all the more gladly about my weaknesses, so that Christ's power may rest on me." 2 Corinthians 12:9

- How can we reveal the character of Christ? *Matthew 5:1–16*
- How did the apostles react? *Acts 5:41*

EXERCISE TAKE THE EIGHT BEATITUDES AND PUT THEM INTO LIFE CIRCUMSTANCES AND DISCUSS HOW THEY WOULD BE EVIDENCED.

Turning Hell into Heaven

Jesus could have turned back from the prospect of hell on the Cross, but because of His unfailing love He has brought heaven to our times.

"_____. But where there are prophecies, they will cease; where there are tongues, they will be stilled; where there is knowledge, it will pass away." 1 Corinthians 13:8

- What two elements reveal Christ's glory? *John 1:14*
- What was Paul's command to the Ephesians? *Ephesians 5:2*

Tick those boxes which your name could honestly be applied to:

... is patient	❏	... does not delight in evil	❏
... is kind	❏	... rejoices with the truth	❏
... does not envy	❏	... always protects	❏
... does not boast	❏	... always trusts	❏
... is not proud	❏	... always hopes	❏
... is not self-seeking	❏	... always perseveres	❏
... is not easily angered	❏		
... keeps no record of wrongs	❏	*(1 Corinthians 13:4–7)*	

Unresolved Conflicts

When unresolved conflicts remain they affect our view of other aspects of life. Instead of praise there arises bitterness and resentment to others.

"*When the disciples James and John saw this, they asked, '____*

_____

_____?' " Luke 9:54

■ What happens when we fail to respond to God's grace? *Hebrews 12:15*

■ What are we to do? *Ephesians 4:31–32*

PAUSE FOR PRAISE SPEND SOME MINUTES PRAISING GOD THAT HE IS USING EVERY SETBACK AS A STEPPING STONE.

Action Plan

Select seven characteristics from the list of 1 Corinthians 13, one for each day. Write them separately on a card for each day and then make that your attitude goal for the day.

Recap

A central truth of the Christian faith is that God can use every setback to be a stepping stone if we respond correctly to it, drawing on the inner strength of God's grace. Jesus was the greatest example of right reactions to life situations. Everything He did was motivated by love, which enabled Him to resolve every conflict in the right way. When this is our experience, praise flows from our hearts and lips.

Developing a Life of Praise

Key Truth

"I will praise you _____ , and in your name I will lift up my hands." **Psalm 63:4**

We have seen that if we are going to enjoy a life of continued praise we must pay attention, not only to our actions, but also to our reactions.

SHARE HOW YOU GOT ON WITH YOUR ACTION PLAN.

Review Wrong Reactions

Spend some time quietly going over your life to see if you are reacting wrongly to life's situations.

"Search me, O God, and know my heart; test me and know my anxious thoughts. _____

_____ and lead me in the way everlasting." Psalm 139:23–24

■ What is a wrong reaction? *1 Peter 3:8–9*

■ What is a right response? *1 Peter 3:8–9*

■ How are we to respond to our enemies? *Romans 12:20*

■ What are we to make sure of? *1 Thessalonians 5:15*

ACTIVITY   GO ROUND THE GROUP ONE AFTER THE OTHER THINKING OF AS MANY WRONG REACTIONS AS YOU CAN UNTIL YOU CAN THINK OF NO MORE — GET SOMEONE TO WRITE THEM DOWN. DO THE SAME WITH RIGHT RESPONSES.

Deal with Wrong Reactions

Be willing to recognise them and not to justify yourself. Admit where you are wrong and confess it, deal with it at the roots.

"Do not be overcome by evil, _____ _____ ." Romans 12:21

■ What must be done to unfruitful roots? *Matthew 3:10*

■ What determines holy branches? *Romans 11:16*

■ What was Paul's prayer? *Ephesians 3:17–18*

■ What causes us to overflow with thankfulness? *Colossians 2:6–7*

PAUSE FOR PRAYER GET A GROUP MEMBER TO READ THE LIST YOU HAVE MADE WHILE THE GROUP IS IN PRAYER. RECOGNISE AND CONFESS IN A MOMENT OF QUIET AND PERSONAL PRAYER ANY THAT APPLY TO YOU.

Don't Stay as You Are

There is something within us that resists change. Our willingness to change into Christlikeness will bring a life of praise through forgiveness.

" _____ _____ for the sake of Christ." Philippians 3:7

■ What did God require of the Children of Israel? *Jeremiah 7:5*

■ What challenge did Jesus give to the disciples? *Matthew 18:3*

■ What did the psalmist ask for? *Psalm 51:12*

THOUGHT GOD LOVES US JUST AS WE ARE, BUT LOVES US TOO MUCH TO LET US STAY AS WE ARE.

Grace Available

In the midst of every storm of life, God's sustaining grace is available to draw upon.

"But he said to me, ' _____ *, for my power is made perfect in weakness'..."*
2 Corinthians 12:9a

Word Study

GRACE: Charis – χάρις (Greek)
The bestowing of pleasure, delight or favourable regard; the expression of loving kindness and goodwill; the supernatural giving of divine spiritual energy to sustain and strengthen.

■ What is guaranteed? *John 16:33*

■ What will come in the morning? *Psalm 30:5*

■ What has God promised? *Isaiah 61:3*

INVITE FROM THE GROUP TESTIMONIES OF TIMES WHEN GOD'S GRACE HAS SUSTAINED THEM.

Be Sensitive to Others

"Praise the Lord" is not a cliché to be foisted on others in their distress. Insensitivity can cause the encouragement to praise to be ill-timed and inappropriate.

"Rejoice with those who rejoice; _____ _____ *."* Romans 12:15

■ What are the strong to do? *Romans 15:1*

■ How do we fulfil the law of Christ? *Galatians 6:2*

THINK THROUGH SOME SITUATIONS WHEN IT WOULD BE INSENSITIVE TO IMPOSE "PRAISE THE LORD" ON OTHERS.

God Loves You

God does not love us because we are thankful, we are thankful because He loves us.

"This is love: not that we loved God, _____ _____ *and sent his Son as an atoning sacrifice for our sins."* 1 John 4:10

■ Why should our praise flow? *Matthew 10:8*

■ Why did the psalmist give thanks? *Psalm 107:1*

SING A SONG **GET THE GROUP TO SING "SUCH LOVE, PURE AS THE WHITEST SNOW".**

Endless Reasons

We are often such thankless people, but when we take time to consider, oh what endless reasons there are to give thanks to a generous God!

"Great is the Lord and _____ ;
his greatness no-one can fathom." Psalm 145:3

■ What is the will of God for us? *1 Thessalonians 5:18*

■ What are we to do always? *Philippians 4:4*

Action Plan

This week write your own psalm of thanksgiving.

Recap

We need to continually review our reactions and deal with wrong ones in order to live the life of praise. God's grace is always available to us, and we need to be gracious to others in their moments of distress. As we perceive God's love our hearts are thankful and magnanimous towards God, because of His continued goodness.

Final Thoughts

We have seen over these studies what an important part praise and worship has in the life of the believer. List the five things that have made the most impact on you during these studies:

_____

_____

_____

_____

_____

Spend the final few moments of these studies giving thanks together in the group.

What is Discipleship?

Key Truth

"... He thus revealed his glory, _____
_____ ." John 2:11b

Throughout the Gospels one term is used more than any other to mark the relationship between Christ and His followers: discipleship. Although we are committed to Christ many of us struggle with the deeper elements of discipleship.

List below what you think discipleship is	What areas do you struggle with?

DISCUSS THIS EXERCISE IN TWOS OR THREES. LIST SOME GOALS YOU HAVE FOR THIS STUDY.

GOALS _____

_____

_____

Tick the statements you agree with:

❑ Discipleship means 'disciplined one'.

❑ Discipleship means the ability to work miracles.

❑ The words 'disciple' and 'Christian' are synonymous.

❑ You can be a believer without being a disciple.

❑ Disciples have public ministries

- ❑ Discipleship means being committed to the authority of another Christian.

- ❑ Disciples live in separate communities to be effective.

- ❑ Disciples are those who acknowledge the Lordship of Christ.

- ❑ 'Disciples' refers only to the twelve Jesus called.

 Practical Tip

People usually do not achieve goals, simply because they do not take time to set them.

 Word Study

DISCIPLE: Mathētēs – μαθητής (Greek)
To learn by following another's teaching; an adherent and imitator of a teacher embracing, imbibing, and acting on these teachings.

Follower

This is someone who is willing to leave what they are doing in order to follow after another.

"To the Jews who had believed him, Jesus said, ' _____

_____

_____*.'"* John 8:31

- ◼ What simple call did Jesus give? *Matthew 4:19–20*

- ◼ What was the only promise that accompanied it? *Matthew 4:19–20*

- ◼ What was the price of following? *Matthew 8:18–22*

DISCUSS **THE IMPLICATIONS OF JESUS' WORDS.**

Learner

This is someone who gives full attention to another in order to receive their teaching.

" 'Take my yoke upon you _____*,
for I am gentle and humble in heart, and you will find rest for your souls.' "* Matthew 11:29

- ◼ What title was given to Jesus? *John 3:2*

- ◼ Why is He the master teacher? *Colossians 2:2–3*

■ What made His teaching different? *Matthew 7:29*

DISCUSS SOME OF THE ELEMENTS THAT ARE PART OF THE LEARNING PROCESS.

For Example:

Takes time _____ _____

Needs application _____ _____

_____ _____

Believer

This is someone who not only embraces an idea but puts their faith in another and commits their life to them.

"This, the first of his miraculous signs, Jesus performed in Cana of Galilee. He thus revealed his glory, _____

_____ ." John 2:11

■ What were they called before Christians? *Acts 11:26*

■ Why were they to praise God? *1 Peter 4:16*

 Word Study

CHRISTIAN: Christianos – χριστιανός (Greek)
A committed follower of Christ; the adjectival termination – 'ianos' – was diffused throughout the whole empire and originally applied to slaves of great households, and was used to denote the adherents to an individual or party.

Finding Identity

A disciple, as he loses his life to his master, takes on his master's identity.

"Whoever finds his life will lose it, and whoever loses his life for my sake _____ ." Matthew 10:39

■ How do we find our identity? *Mark 8:35*

■ How did Paul put it? *Philippians 3:8*

■ Why did Jesus know who He was? *John 13:3*

PAUSE FOR THOUGHT HOW DOES A DISCIPLE RESPOND TO THE QUESTION, "WHO AM I?"

Maintaining Uniqueness

In discipling, God never loses sight of the uniqueness of our individual self.

" _____ , *created in Christ Jesus to do good works, which God prepared in advance for us to do.*" Ephesians 2:10

■ What is the Bible truth about individuality? *Psalm 139:13–16*

■ How is our value viewed? *Matthew 10:31*

One of the greatest gaps that exists in the Church today is between belief and behaviour. We have been telling people what to do but not teaching them how. We have looked at the five characteristics of a disciple. List the expected behaviour patterns.

Belief	Behaviour of
Follower	
Learner	
Believer	
Identity in Christ	
Uniqueness of	

Action Plan

Find another Christian this week and ask them to explain to you what a disciple is, and share with them your own understanding of the word.

Recap

A disciple of Christ is one who follows after Christ, embraces His teaching, commits his entire life to Christ and finds his full identity in Christ through the uniqueness of his own personality.

Becoming a Disciple

Key Truth

" 'Suppose one of you wants to build a tower. _____

_____

to see if he has enough money to complete it?' " Luke 14:28

Last week we looked at what discipleship is and now we move on to see how we join the school of discipleship, but first discuss how you got on with your action plan.

Surrender

The foundation stone of discipleship is our willingness to surrender our own desires.

"My son, _____
and let your eyes keep to my ways ..." Proverbs 23:26

■ What is the real meaning of Jesus' apparently harsh words in *Luke 14:25–27?*

■ Why did the young man struggle with the call to discipleship? *Matthew 19:21–22*

■ What challenge did Jesus present? *Luke 14:28–35*

■ What was Peter able to say? *Luke 18:28–29*

DISCUSS THE IMPLICATIONS OF THESE CHALLENGING STATEMENTS.

Repentance

Repentance is the primary plank over which everyone must walk if they are to become a disciple.

" *'I have not come to call the righteous, but sinners*

_____ *.' ''*

Luke 5:32

■ What was John's message? *Matthew 3:1–2*

■ What did Peter preach? *Acts 2:38*

 Practical Tip
The key to repentance is agreeing with God –
You are right, I am wrong, I will do what You
say.

■ What needs to accompany repentance?
2 Corinthians 7:9–10

■ How did Jesus emphasise repentance? *Luke 9:62*

 Word Study
REPENTANCE: Metanoeō – μετανοέω (Greek)
A complete change of mind that leads to a
complete change of direction, that leads to a
complete change in behaviour, through submission of the will.

TO THINK THROUGH IS REPENTANCE A ONE-
OFF EXPERIENCE OR AN ONGOING PROCESS?

Self-Interest

The thing that militates most against our commitment to discipleship is our own self-interest.

"*Those who belong to Christ Jesus* _____

_____

_____ *.* ''

Galatians 5:24

- What does self-interest make us do? *Luke 14:16–20*

- What are we to do with self-interest?
Matthew 16:24–26

- What is the root of all sin? *Isaiah 14:13–14*

- How did Jesus challenge self-interest? *Luke 9:57–62*

List some of the self-interests we often pursue:

_____

_____

_____

_____

New Birth

The beginning of a life of discipleship begins with the wonder of the new birth.

"_____,
*not of perishable seed, but of imperishable, through the living
and enduring word of God.*" 1 Peter 1:23

- What did Nicodemus acknowledge? *John 3:2*

- Where did Jesus start with His call to discipleship?
John 3:4–15

TALK THROUGH **THE POPULAR USAGE OF THE
TERM "BORN AGAIN".**

Lordship of Christ

The importance of accepting the Lordship of Christ is the basis of our willingness to walk in obedience in His ways.

"*Therefore let all Israel be assured of this: God has made
this Jesus, whom you crucified,*_____

_____." Acts 2:36

- How did Thomas respond? *John 20:28*

- Why did Christ die and be raised to new life?
Romans 14:9

- What does Jesus have? *Colossians 1:15–20*

Radical Obedience

If this world is to be changed, Jesus needs men and women who will not easily give up in order to do their own thing.

" *'My sheep listen to my voice; I know them, _____ .' "*

John 10:27

■ What is the evidence of discipleship? *John 14:15–23*

■ What solemn words did Jesus utter? *Matthew 7:21*

■ How did Peter and the apostles display discipleship? *Acts 5:29*

 Practical Tip
Jesus sets the standards high, but always remember He has promised to supply the power to achieve them.

THINK OF OTHER BIBLE PASSAGES ON THIS ISSUE.

Action Plan

This week keep a daily journal. At the end of each day ask yourself these three questions and then jot down the answers:

■ What did I do today in the interest of Christ?

■ What did I do today in the interest of others?

■ What did I do today in the interest of myself?

If there is an imbalance, seek to correct it as you progress through the week.

Recap

Becoming a disciple means surrendering my will in repentance to Christ and experiencing the new birth. Being willing to turn from my self-interest and to come and submit myself to Christ in radical obedience.

The Discipline of Discipleship

Key Truth

"... for acquiring a _____
_____ , doing what is right and just and fair." Proverbs 1:3

Discipline is an important ingredient of discipleship. It can sound grim or foreboding but let us not draw back, as it is an essential element of effective discipleship which builds character. Explore with each other the comments you recorded in your daily journal last week.

Self-Control

A disciple regards the issue of personal accountability seriously and takes responsibility for his own actions.

"... and to knowledge, _____
_____ ; and to perseverance, godliness ..." 2 Peter 1:6

■ What is a man who lacks self-control like? *Proverbs 25:28*

■ What is the key to self-control? *Galatians 5:22–23*

■ What accompanies self-control? *1 Peter 4:7*

TO LEARN **WHAT DO WE NEED TO LEARN FROM THESE PASSAGES?**

Freedom of Choice

This does not mean that all restraints are now disregarded because we are under grace.

"... because through Christ Jesus _____
_____
free from the law of sin and death." Romans 8:2

■ What must we be careful of? *1 Corinthians 8:9*

■ What do we often indulge in under the guise of freedom *Galatians 5:13*

It means that we live freely within the boundaries of Christ's teaching.

■ What should we not use our freedom as? *1 Peter 2:16*

■ What two things did Paul differentiate between? *1 Corinthians 10:23, 6:12.*

 Practical Tip

It is better to build a fence at the top of a hill than a hospital at the bottom.

THINK OF SOME EXAMPLES OF THINGS WHICH ARE PERMISSIBLE, BUT NOT BENEFICIAL, AND DISCUSS THEM WITH YOUR GROUP.

E.g. It is permissible to dress in the way that you choose, it is not beneficial to dress in such a way that provokes others wrongly.

The Will of God

Part of the process of discipline is applying ourselves to discover the will of God and then committing ourselves to it.

" ' _____, your law is within my heart.' " Psalm 40:8

■ What was the psalmist's request? *Psalm 143:10*

■ How are we to do the will of God? *Ephesians 6:6*

■ What is our spiritual act of worship, and how does it relate to the will of God? *Romans 12:1–2*

THINK THROUGH WHAT IS THE RELATIONSHIP BETWEEN THE REVEALED WILL OF GOD (WORD OF GOD) AND THE UNREVEALED WILL OF GOD.

Spiritual Surgery

When we recognise areas of our lives that are not consistent with that of a disciple, we need to take action accordingly.

"No, _____ so that after I have preached to others, I myself will not be disqualified for the prize." 1 Corinthians 9:27

■ What challenging truth did Jesus teach? *Matthew 5:30*

■ What is our first responsibility? *Matthew 7:4–5*

■ Who does the purifying? *2 Corinthians 7:1*

ARE THERE AREAS OF MY LIFE THAT NEED SPIRITUAL SURGERY?

Pause for personal prayer.

Fear of the Lord

We can respond to discipline out of fear of punishment, rewards gained by obedience, or out of love and respect.

"Who, then, _____?
He will instruct him in the way chosen for him."
Psalm 25:12

■ Where does wisdom begin? *Psalm 111:10*

■ What is stored up for those who fear the Lord? *Psalm 31:19*

■ What is "reverent fear"? *1 Peter 1:17*

 Word Study

FEAR (of the Lord): Eulabeia – εὐλάβεια (Greek) To approach with a sense of caution, awe and reverence; a holy apprehension that indicates piety and respect mingled with deep love.

Relationship Precedes Rules

Our relationship with God is that of sons and daughters. His disciplines are lovingly and tenderly worked out and produce growth and maturity.

" '_____ you will obey what I command.' " John 14:15

■ How are we to respond to discipline? *Proverbs 3:11–12*

■ What does discipline bring? *Psalm 94:12*

■ What motivates discipline? *Revelation 3:19*

 Practical Tip

Rules without relationship produce rebellion.

THINK THROUGH THE ELEMENTS OF RE-
LATIONSHIP AND WHAT IMPACT THEY HAVE IN
THE APPLICATION OF RULES.

Relationship	Rules

Example:
    Love
    Understanding
	Just
	Fair

Discipline, a Pattern of Life

When we take time to implement structured discipline it becomes internalised and self-discipline flows out through discipleship.

" *'A student is not above his teacher, but everyone who is fully trained* _____ *.'* " Luke 6:40

■ What were the Philippians to continue to do? *Philippians 2:12–13*

■ What was Paul's word to Timothy? *2 Timothy 1:13–14*

■ What was Paul able to say? *Philippians 3:17*

■ What does discipline produce? *Hebrews 12:11*

Action Plan

Take time to review your lifestyle during the next week. Use the permissible/non-beneficial chart. Face firmly any areas of indiscipline by changing your pattern of life in that area.

Recap

The life of a disciple is a disciplined one – exercising self-control and freedom within the context of Christ's teachings. With awe, respect and deep love disciples apply themselves to the will of God, dealing firmly with issues as they arise – taking the appropriate action to rectify them. The result is a pattern of life that is disciplined, not simply obeying rules but enjoying a deep relationship.

Discipleship Builds Character

Key Truth

"... your salvation with fear and trembling, for it is God who works in you to will and to act according to his good purpose."
Philippians 2:12b–13

Although disciple means learner, it does not mean that we just sit like students in the classroom storing up facts and information, but each truth Christ unfolds has to be lived out in practical life situations.

The Crucible of Circumstances

When God wants to develop an aspect of our character, He allows a circumstance that will develop it.

"But he knows the way that I take; when _____
_____."

Job 23:10

■ How are we to respond to life's circumstances?
  James 1:2

■ Why? *James 1:3*

■ What is the result? *James 1:4*

List some of the circumstances God allows and the characteristic it produces:

Circumstance	Characteristic
Example: Confusion Hurt by others	Trust Forgiveness

A Person Not a Principle

We are not to be legalists following the letter of the law, but followers of Christ drawing on His resurrection life within.

" _____

_____, And I pray that you, being rooted and established in love ..._" Ephesians 3:17

■ What is "the hope of glory"? _Colossians 1:27_

■ What was Paul able to say? _Galatians 2:20_

■ Who is God's power for? _Ephesians 1:19–20_

DISCUSS THE CHARACTERISTICS OF CHRIST'S LIFE.

Bad Habits

Wrong habits must be recognised, faced and dealt with through repentance and a change of will through surrendering it to Christ.

"As a result, he does not live the rest of his earthly life

_____,

but rather for the will of God." 1 Peter 4:2

■ What are we to do with the old self? _Ephesians 4:22_

■ What must we rid ourselves of? _Colossians 3:5–10_

■ What have we spent enough time doing?
1 Peter 4:1–3

Good Habits

It is possible to establish good habits by continually practising them until they become second nature.

" 'The good man brings _____

_____, ...' "
Matthew 12:35a

■ What should we make every effort to do?
2 Peter 1:5–9

■ What is a good habit to develop? _Philippians 4:8_

┌───┐
│ **P** **Practical Tip** │
│ **If you do something regularly for 30 days it will** │
│ **become a habit – make sure it is a good one.** │
└───┘

■ What will good habits do? *1 Thessalonians 4:11–12*

MAKE A LIST OF WHAT YOU CONSIDER TO BE GOOD HABITS AND BAD HABITS.

An Organised Life

Discipleship involves the right use of time and resources. Not wasting or squandering either.

"Live life, then, with a due sense of responsibility ... Make _____ , despite all the evils of these days." Ephesians 5:15–16 (J. B. Phillips)

■ What leads to instability? *James 1:8*

■ Who sets a good example? *Proverbs 6:6–11*

MAKE A TIME CHART LIKE THE ONE ON PAGE 14, TO COVER EVERY HOUR OF YOUR WEEK.

Fill in the spaces indicating exactly what you did for each hour period. The purpose of this exercise is to help you to see where your time is spent in an average week.

Learning from the Word

Show me a disciple and I will show you a person who spends time with the Word. He ponders it, prays over it, and meditates on it as much as he is able.

"Do your best to present yourself to God as one approved, a workman who does not need to be ashamed and _____ _____."

2 Timothy 2:15

■ What did Paul write to the Colossians? *Colossians 3:16*

■ What did Jesus say about His Word? *John 6:63*

■ What did David do with the Word? *Psalm 119:11*

Practical Tip

Meditate on God's Word just before you go to sleep at night – the last thoughts in our mind remain active while we sleep.

CHALLENGE GO ROUND THE GROUP AND SEE HOW MANY BIBLE VERSES CAN BE QUOTED FROM MEMORY.

A Courageous Heart

Many issues of life demand great courage. The disciple draws from the wisdom and strength of his Master and with courage chooses that which is right.

"When I called, you answered me; _____

_____ ." Psalm 138:3

■ What are the righteous like? *Proverbs 28:1*

■ What did Peter and John display? *Acts 4:13*

■ What did the believers pray? *Acts 4:29-31*

■ What was the result of Paul's chains? *Philippians 1:14*

Action Plan

This week decide on a new good habit to embrace and begin to implement it. Commit yourself to persist in it for the next 30 days. Spend a few minutes thinking about it now and share it with the group.

Recap

The circumstances of life build character as we respond to them with the Christ life. That character enables us to build good habits and discard bad ones, effectively using our time and resources wisely. As we spend disciplined time in the Word, we receive great wisdom, strength and courage to choose to do that which is right and godly.

Discipleship: An Ongoing Process

Key Truth
"So then, just as you received Christ Jesus as Lord, _____
_____ ..." **Colossians 2:6**

The school of discipleship is deeply challenging and often affects our comfort zones. At these moments there is the opportunity to turn back, but the true disciple echoes the words of Peter, "Lord, to whom shall we go? You have the words of eternal life." Share with each other how you are getting on with your new habits.

Maintaining a Tender Heart

Because of the pressures and harsh experiences of life, it is easy for our hearts to become calloused and hard.

"But they refused to pay attention; _____
_____
_____ ."* Zechariah 7:11

■ Why must we encourage each other daily?
Hebrews 3:13

■ What does "break up your unploughed ground" mean? *Hosea 10:12*

■ What did God promise? *Ezekiel 36:26–27*

Word Study
HEART: Kardia – καρδία (Greek)
Represents man's entire mental, moral, rational and emotional activity. It is used figuratively for the hidden springs of the personal life and functioning.

An All Consuming Heart

When we are willing to pull down all barriers preventing the flow of Christ's love, we will experience a love that allows no other rivals to occupy the centre of our hearts.

" _____ ,
because we are convinced that one died for all, and therefore all died." 2 Corinthians 5:14

■ What militates against love? *1 Corinthians 13:11*

■ What did Paul do about it? *1 Corinthians 13:11*

■ How do men know we are disciples? *John 13:35*

LIST AND DISCUSS SOME OF THE CHILDISH BEHAVIOUR PATTERNS THAT WORK AGAINST LOVE.

Example:

Getting my own way _____   _____

Getting my own back _____   _____

_____   _____

A Joyful Exchange

This is the experience of willingly giving up our rights to all that is our own, and becoming a steward rather than a proprietor. A release of joy ensues as the burden is lifted.

" '*If you obey my commands, you will remain in my love, just as I have obeyed my Father's commands and remain in his love. I have told you this so that* _____
_____ .' "
John 15:10–11

■ Why did Jesus endure the cross? *Hebrews 12:2*

■ How is our burden lightened? *Matthew 11:28–30*

■ What is the kingdom of God a matter of? *Romans 14:17*

TO PONDER ON "IF YOU OWN SOMETHING THAT YOU COULD NOT GIVE AWAY, YOU DON'T OWN IT, IT OWNS YOU." ALBERT SCHWEITZER

■ What are the implications of this statement?

A Servant Heart

We are called as disciples to serve. The characteristic of a servant is not a competitive or an egocentric spirit, but one of humility.

"_____ as if you were serving the Lord, not men, ..._" Ephesians 6:7

■ What are we to clothe ourselves with? *1 Peter 5:5*

■ How did Jesus describe greatness? *Matthew 18:4*

■ How did Jesus respond to the disciples? *Luke 22:24–26*

LIST SOME ELEMENTS OF SERVANTHOOD.

Example:

Willingness _____

Industrious _____

_____ _____

Baptism

Jesus commanded that those who become His disciples should be baptised. The command of the Lord is as valid today as when He gave the great command.

" 'Therefore go and make disciples of all nations,_____

_____

_____, ...' " Matthew 28:19

■ What example did Jesus set? *Matthew 3:13–17*

■ What is the significance of baptism? *Romans 6:1–4*

■ What did the eunuch ask? *Acts 8:36–38*

TO PONDER HAVE I BEEN BAPTISED?

Communion

Through the simple yet profound meal of bread and wine we are brought into an attitude of the deepest reverence, to worship and adore the One we love and serve.

"_____
_____
_____
_____
_____? Because there is one loaf, we, who are many, are one body, for we all partake of the one loaf._"
1 Corinthians 10:16–17

■ What is the covenant? *Matthew 26:28*

■ How should we approach the communion table? *1 Corinthians 11:23–32*

■ What should we do before we come to the altar? *Matthew 5:23–24*

TO DO MAKE SURE YOU PARTICIPATE IN THE NEXT CHURCH CELEBRATION OF COMMUNION.

Action Plan

Decide on two things to do this week for others that will display a servant heart and attitude.

Recap

Discipleship is an ongoing process that necessitates the maintaining of a tender and passionate heart towards the Lord, and a willingness to be a servant – not holding on to my rights but surrendering them to His will. Discipleship also involves an outward public proclamation through baptism and regular sharing with other disciples in the celebration of the Communion service.

Disciples Who Make An Impact

Key Truth

"He said to them, ' _____

_____ .' " **Mark 16:15**

In a few short years the disciples established the Christian Church as a major focus in the world.

Not to be Ignored

It seems that wherever the early disciples went there was either a revival or a riot.

"… and repentance and forgiveness of sins _____

_____ ."

Luke 24:47

■ What did they say about the early disciples? *Acts 2:13*

■ What else did they say? *Acts 17:6*

■ What impact did they have? *Acts 3:11–12*

DISCUSS WHY YOU THINK THE CHURCH IS LARGELY BEING IGNORED TODAY.

Submission to Spiritual Authority

Each of us needs to be in submission to some spiritual authority. To do so puts us under a covering that protects us and helps us to live lives free from strain and anxiety.

"_____

_____. They keep watch over you as men who must give an account. Obey them so that their work will be a joy, not a burden, for that would be of no advantage to you." Hebrews 13:17

■ What was Paul's directive to the Corinthians?
  1 Corinthians 16:16–17

■ How are we to respond to the elders? *1 Peter 5:1–7*

■ How are we to relate to each other? *Ephesians 5:21*

THINK OF OTHER SCRIPTURES THAT SHOW WHAT OTHER AUTHORITY STRUCTURES GOD HAS PUT AROUND US.

Anointed by the Spirit

When the Holy Spirit descended He set the disciples on fire; they were spiritual incendiaries blazing the gospel trail.

" *'If you then, though you are evil, know how to give good gifts to your children, how much more will your Father in heaven*

_____

_____ *!'* " Luke 11:13

■ What had Joel prophesied? *Joel 2:28–29*

■ What did John say of Jesus? *Matthew 3:11*

■ What was Peter's reply? *Acts 2:38*

Flowing in the Power of Resurrection Life

The hallmark of the early disciples was that Christ lived in them, moved in them, worked, thought and ministered His life through them.

"Jesus answered, ' _____

_____ *. No-one comes to the Father except through me.'* " John 14:6

■ Who did Jesus declare He was? *John 11:25*

■ What is abundant life? *John 10:10*

■ How do we know He lives in us? *1 John 3:24*

Word Study

LIFE:
Bios – βίος **(Greek)**
The manner of life and how we live it; our every day living and means of life.
Psuchē – ψυχή **(Greek)**
Our natural life and the source of our inner life of thought, feeling and decision.
Zōē – ζωή **(Greek)**
Life as it can only be found and experienced in God. That life which only comes out of God Himself.

Unsatisfied Satisfaction

The amazing thing about being a disciple is that the more we receive of Christ and are blessed, the more we want.

"_____,
_____ *so that your youth is renewed like the eagle's.*" Psalm 103:5

■ What did Jesus promise? *Matthew 5:6*

■ What did Paul disclose? *Philippians 3:10–11*

■ How did the psalmist put it? *Psalm 42:1–2*

DISCUSS WHAT YOU THINK IT IS THAT THOSE WHO DO NOT KNOW CHRIST THIRST FOR.

LIST SOME OF THE WAYS IN WHICH THEY SEEK TO SATISFY THEIR THIRST ...

Example:

Career _____ _____

Getting married _____ _____

_____ _____

Not Always Popular

As a disciple we can expect pressure from society. A true Christian witness will always evoke a response. Sometimes it will be antagonistic. Remember our forefathers died for their faith.

"In fact, everyone who wants to live a godly life in Christ Jesus —————————— persecuted ..." 2 Timothy 3:12

■ Who was Saul really persecuting? *Acts 9:4–5*

■ How are we to respond to persecution? *Matthew 5:11–12*

■ What did Jesus say? *Matthew 10:22*

CHALLENGE WHEN WAS THE LAST TIME YOU SUFFERED PERSECUTION FOR BEING A DISCIPLE?

Action Plan

Spend some moments together asking God to fill you with His Holy Spirit.

Recap

The early disciples were not people who could be ignored. Having been impacted by the resurrection life of Christ and empowered by the Holy Spirit, they functioned under spiritual authority. Although they were considerably persecuted it did not quell their thirst for more of the Christ life.

Final Thoughts

We have seen in this six week study that God calls us not just to salvation but to discipleship.

List the main things you have learned about discipleship in this study:

———————————————————————

———————————————————————

———————————————————————

———————————————————————

Spend a few moments in prayer, re-dedicating yourself to be an effective disciple of Christ.

What are Relationships?

Key Truth

"_____, because they have a good return for their work: If one falls down, his friend can help him up. But pity the man who falls and has no-one to help him up!"
Ecclesiastes 4:9–10

John Wesley said that he was "a man sent from God to persuade people to put Christ at the centre of their relationships". It is true to say that most of our problems in life arise from an inability to relate effectively to others. If we do not know how to relate well, we do not know how to live, for as someone has put it, "to be, is to be in relationship".

LIST ON A SHEET OF PAPER SOME OF THE DIFFICULTIES THAT ARISE IN RELATIONSHIPS AND THE WAYS WE LEARN TO HANDLE THEM.

SHARE YOUR CONCLUSIONS WITH THE GROUP AND ESTABLISH SOME GOALS FOR THIS STUDY.

GOALS _____

_____

_____

WRITE OUT YOUR DEFINITION OF THE PERFECT RELATIONSHIP:

_____

_____

_____

■ What is the purpose of relationships? (See next page)

❏ to have a companion   Add others to the list:
❏ so my needs can be met   ❏ _____
❏ to avoid loneliness   ❏ _____
❏ for procreation   ❏ _____
❏ to have help at hand   ❏ _____
❏ to do things together
❏ to please God

Number them in order of priority.

DISCUSS YOUR DEFINITION AND CONCLUSIONS WITH THE GROUP.

Early Relationships

The first relationships we experience are in the home. These first relationships powerfully shape the image we have of ourselves, which in turn influences how we relate to people as we go through life.

" 'A new command I give you: Love one another. As I have loved you, _____ .' " John 13:34

◼ What are some of the relational characteristics of love? *1 Corinthians 13:4–6*

◼ What militates against them? *1 Corinthians 13:11*

◼ Why did Paul admonish the Corinthians? *1 Corinthians 14:20*

DISCUSS WHAT PAUL WAS TEACHING HERE.

Word Study
PUT AWAY: Katargeō – καταργέω **(Greek)**
To make to cease; to do away with; to render inoperative; to completely cut off; put an end to.

Home is Not Just a Place

Both mother and father play significant and much needed roles in a child's life.

"Jesus replied, 'If anyone loves me, he will obey my teaching. _____ , and we will come to him and make our home with him.' " John 14:23

◼ Why was the Lord with Jehoshaphat? *2 Chronicles 17:3–4*

◼ What was Paul's observation of Timothy? *2 Timothy 1:5*

■ What is said of Ahaziah? *1 Kings 22:52; 2 Chronicles 22:3*

LIST SOME OF THE EARLY INFLUENCES OF YOUR HOME THAT AFFECT YOU TODAY:

Early experiences	How they affect you today
E.g. Dad was never there Dad always made time for us	

SHARE SOME OF THEM WITH THE GROUP.

 Practical Tip

When disciplining children it is best not to use the hand for punishment, i.e. slapping. The hand should be for blessing and support and encouragement. The Bible always refers to an independent implement as a means of correction.

Discipline Wrapped in Love

The way discipline is applied in the home greatly influences the way a child relates to itself and others.

"Folly is bound up in the heart of a child, _____ _____ ." Proverbs 22:15

■ What is the difference between training and discipline? *Proverbs 22:6*

■ What does a loving Father do? *Deuteronomy 4:9*

DISCUSS THE RELATIONSHIP BETWEEN LOVE AND DISCIPLINE.

Our First Concept of God

Early relationships become the great window through which we develop our view of heavenly things.

"Jesus answered: 'Don't you know me, Philip, even after I have been among you such a long time? _____ _____

How can you say, "Show us the Father?"' " John 14:9

■ What could be an answer to Isaiah's question? *Isaiah 40:18*

■ What was Paul able to say? *1 Corinthians 4:16*

LIST ON A SEPARATE SHEET SOME WAYS OUR PARENTS MODEL A CONCEPT OF GOD:

Positive	Negative
E.g. Caring Warm	E.g. Authoritarian Punitive

DISCUSS WITH THE GROUP.

Our Relational Style

It is from our early relationships that we develop what might be called our relational style – a way of relating to others that best suits us.

"*Therefore, as God's chosen people, holy and dearly loved, clothe yourselves* _____

_____.*" Colossians 3:12

■ What is a wrong relational style? *Proverbs 24:29*

■ What is a good relational style? *1 Peter 3:9*

■ What was Paul's relational style? *1 Corinthians 4:14–15*

DISCUSS WHAT MOTIVATES US TO MOVE IN THE THREE RELATIONAL STYLES MENTIONED IN THE DAILY READINGS.

Action Plan

This week explain to a close friend what relational style means and ask them how they observe your relational style towards others. Be willing to listen to what they say.

Recap

Our early relationships in the family prepare us for future life encounters. Our parents' influence affects us greatly, especially the way they disciplined us, and from this early influence our concept of God and of ourselves has been shaped. Out of these early developmental years our relational style has been developed.

Maturing in Relationships

Key Truth

"May the Lord make your _____

_____ ,

just as ours does for you." I Thessalonians 3:12

We mature to the degree that we know how to relate to God, ourselves and to others. The immature person retreats in on himself, withdraws from relationships and becomes self pre-occupied. The result of sin is that it brings estrangement – estrangement from God, estrangement from ourselves and estrangement from others.

SHARE HOW YOU GOT ON WITH YOUR ACTION PLAN AND SEE IF YOU LEARNED ANYTHING ABOUT YOUR RELATIONAL STYLE.

A Sign of Maturity

Mature people are loosed from self-centred pre-occupation and enter into fellowship with God and others.

"But if we walk in the light, as he is in the light, _____

_____ , and the blood of Jesus, his Son, purifies us from all sin." 1 John 1:7

■ What is the fruit of a mature personality? *1 John 3:16–18*

■ What is the royal law? *James 2:8*

■ What is the new commandment? *John 13:34*

■ How was immaturity displayed? *Luke 15:28–30*

LIST WHAT YOU CONSIDER TO BE THE EVIDENCE OF MATURITY AND IMMATURITY:

Maturity	Immaturity
E.g. Accepting responsibility for my actions	Impossible behaviour

DISCUSS WITH THE GROUP.

The Heart of Christianity

The quality of relationships found in Christianity is unique because they began with God's initiative towards us at the Cross.

"This is how we know what love is: _____. And we ought to lay down our lives for our brothers." 1 John 3:16

■ How did God demonstrate His deepest desire for relationship? *Galatians 4:4–5; Romans 5:7–8*

■ What is God's order for relationship? *Revelation 1:5b*

■ How do we often reverse this? *Revelation 1:5b*

DISCUSS THE RELATIONSHIP BETWEEN ACCEPTANCE AND LOVE.

Two Sides of the Coin

A good relationship with others flows out of a good relationship with God. Jesus makes it clear that love for God is to be manifested by love for man.

"He answered: ' "Love the Lord your God with all your heart and with all your soul and with all your strength and with all your mind"; and, " _____ *."' "* Luke 10:27

■ Who is your neighbour? *Luke 10:29–30*

■ Did Jesus call him a "good" Samaritan? *Luke 10:33*

■ Where do relationships begin? *Luke 6:38; Acts 20:35*

LIST **THE PRACTICAL DEMONSTRATIONS OF LOVE SHOWN BY THE SAMARITAN.**

The Beginnings of Love

Once we open ourselves to contemplating how much God loves us we open ourselves to receiving that love, and that inflow in turn produces love in us.

"We love _____ *"* 1 John 4:19

■ What is the quality of this love? *Jeremiah 31:3*

■ What does the 'but' declare? *Ephesians 2:4–5*

■ What was Paul's prayer for the Ephesians? *Ephesians 3:14–21*

Word Study

LOVE:

Agapaō – ἀγαπάω (Greek)
Love being the essential nature of God; the divine attitude of deep consuming care and concern, as expressed through great devotion and sacrifice; totally unselfish love.

Phileō – φιλέω (Greek)
Tender affection of one human for another; friendship based on having common interests; to befriend and show a definite interest in someone.

Contemplating the Cross

Without a realisation of how much we are loved, we will try to earn and gain God's love and approval. There is only one way to love God and that is to let Him first love you, by coming and sitting afresh at the foot of the Cross.

" _____ ,
because we are convinced that one died for all, and therefore all died." 2 Corinthians 5:14

■ How much does God love you? *Psalm 139:13–18*

■ How does Paul depict God's love? *Colossians 1:15–23; Philippians 2:6–11*

PAUSE FOR PRAYER GET THE GROUP TO CLOSE THEIR EYES IN AN ATTITUDE OF PRAYER AND ASK THE HOLY SPIRIT TO ILLUMINATE YOUR HEARTS. THE LEADER SHOULD THEN READ JOHN19:28–37.

Action Plan

This week choose someone you would describe as a neighbour. Following the example of the Samaritan, decide on several practical things you will do during the week for them as a practical expression of God's love.

Recap

Good relationships are a sure sign of spiritual maturity. That maturity begins through a deep relationship with God as we recognise His great love for us. As we open ourselves afresh to an inflow of His love by coming again to the Cross, and seeing just how much He loves us, we can reach out to others with that great love.

The Purpose of Living

Key Truth

" 'For I know the plans I have for you,' declares the Lord, 'plans to prosper you and not to harm you, _____

_____ .' "   Jeremiah 29:11

Having looked in the past two weeks at the first of the two highest commandments, "Love the Lord your God with all your heart ...", we turn this week to consider the second: "Love your neighbour as yourself."

How did you get on with your Action Plan and how did your neighbour respond?

The Royal Law

The phrase "as yourself" is important. The love and regard we are to have for others is a reflection of the love and regard we have for our own well-being, not more or less, but in proportion to it.

"If you really keep the royal law found in Scripture, '_____
_____ ' you are doing right."
James 2:8

■ How are we to think of ourselves? *Romans 12:3*

■ How are we to think of others? *Romans 12:10*

■ What are we to look to? *Philippians 2:3–4*

■ How does Paul relate the royal law to marriage? *Ephesians 5:33*

DISCUSS WHAT AN INFERIORITY COMPLEX IS.

Love One Another

To love one another is not always an easy task, but Jesus did not just command it, He demonstrated it. "As I have loved you" was not just His teaching but His lifestyle.

" *'A new command I give you:* _____
_____ *, so you must love one another.' "*
John 13:34

■ How are we to love one another? *1 Peter 1:22*

■ What does this demonstrate? *John 13:35*

■ What must love be? *Romans 12:9*

 SOME OF THE WAYS WE CAN EVIDENCE LOVE FOR EACH OTHER:

E.g. Speak well of each other
_____
_____
_____
_____

P Practical Tip

Develop the principle of the good report. Whenever you speak of others determine that you will speak well of them (though without inventing untrue compliments just to flatter). The human tendency is always to dwell on the negative.

Perfect Love

The love of Christ is the purest and most potent power in the universe. Jesus made love central in His own life and in all His relationships with others.

"
_____
We have seen his glory, the glory of the One and Only, who came from the Father, full of grace and truth." John 1:14

■ What are we to clothe ourselves with? *Colossians 3:12–14*

■ What is the result of perfect love? *1 John 4:18*

LIST SOME OF THE CHARACTERISTICS OF IMPERFECT LOVE:

E.g. Self-centredness

_____

_____

_____

The Meaning of Life

When we experience God's love flowing into the core of our beings we are able to relay that love to others, bringing about the purpose of living – "to love as we are loved."

"*Love does no harm to its neighbour.* _____

_____." Romans 13:10

■ What was Paul's exhortation? *Ephesians 5:2*

■ What ministry has God given us? *2 Corinthians 5:16–21*

■ What did Jesus command His disciples to do? *John 15:9*

DISCUSS HOW RECONCILIATION IS RELATIONAL.

 Word Study

RECONCILIATION:
Katallassō – καταλλάσσω (Greek)
To change from enmity to friendship, evidenced through grace, mercy and forgiveness;
a change in one party induced by the action of another.

The Core Issue

Most problems that we experience in the Christian life stem from a violation of the law of love. We have been failed in love, and therefore we fail in loving others.

"*May the Lord make your love increase and overflow for each other* _____,
just as ours does for you." 1 Thessalonians 3:12

■ What are some of the characteristics of Christ's love for His Church? *Ephesians 5:22–23*

■ How does Paul depict violations of the law of love? *Ephesians 4:31*

■ How are we to deal with them? *Ephesians 4:32*

DISCUSS WHAT "TO LOVE AS WE HAVE BEEN LOVED" MEANS. THINK OF SOME INSTANCES OF ITS OUTWORKING IN CHRIST'S LIFE.

The Sin of Self-Protection

The fear of being hurt, misunderstood, unappreciated or rejected keeps many of us from getting further involved with people. Because we want to protect ourselves we build a protective wall around ourselves.

"... idolatry and witchcraft; hatred, discord, jealousy, fits of rage, _____, dissensions, factions ..."
Galatians 5:20

■ Why did Adam hide? *Genesis 3:10*

■ How did Adam protect himself? *Genesis 3:12*

■ When are we foolish? *Proverbs 28:26*

DISCUSS WHETHER SELF-PROTECTION IS A BASIC INSTINCT OR A SIN.

Action Plan

This week prayerfully consider whether or not there are those you need to be reconciled to, and begin to ask God to help you face the issue.

Recap

We are to fulfil the royal law, having a healthy respect for ourselves, by loving others with the same regard and care as we have for ourselves. The meaning of life, as Christ demonstrated with perfect love, is to love others as we have been loved. Often because we have been hurt by others we do not fulfil the meaning of life but protect ourselves from the possibility of further hurt.

Relational Style

Key Truth

"... even as I try to please everybody in every way. _____

_____ ,

so that they may be saved." I Corinthians 10:33

Self-protection is a category of sin that is often not recognised in the Christian Church. Yet it is the attitude that prefers withdrawal because of the possibility of rejection and pain, rather than taking the risk of involvement. We prefer the safety of self-protection to the risk of loving.

Other-Centredness

The mark of a Christian is a quality of love that directs more energy towards others' concerns than towards one's own well-being.

"*Nobody should seek his own good,* _____

_____ *.*" 1 Corinthians 10:24

■ What did Jesus say is the evidence of discipleship? *John 13:31–38*

■ What are we to do? *Hebrews 13:1–3*

■ What are we to offer? *1 Peter 4:8–10*

THINK OF SOME OTHER CATEGORIES AS WELL AS THOSE MENTIONED IN 1 PETER.

E.g. Strangers, those in prison, those ill-treated

 ## Practical Tip

Remember the smile on someone else's face is usually a reflection of the smile on your own. Be friendly!

Deep Disappointment

The pain of profound disappointment becomes a barrier to a clear and open relationship with God and others. It causes us to react and protect ourselves from further possibility of disappointment.

"A man's spirit sustains him in sickness, but _____ _____ ?" Proverbs 18:14

■ What was the psalmist's lament? *Psalm 41:9, 38:11*

■ What was the psalmist's observation? *Psalm 22:5*

■ What is the antidote to disappointment? *Romans 5:3–5*

LIST SOME OF THE DISAPPOINTMENTS IN RELATIONSHIPS WE OFTEN FACE:

E.g. let down by others _____ _____

_____ _____

PAUSE FOR PRAYER SPEND SOME MOMENTS BRINGING DISAPPOINTMENTS TO THE LORD.

Be Nice to Me

Behind a façade of friendliness can be a desire to please others, so that they in turn will be kind to us and make us feel good. Shyness could be a means to keep us from looking foolish.

"... _____ , because the Day will bring it to light. It will be revealed with fire, and the fire will test the quality of each man's work." 1 Corinthians 3:13

■ What advice did David give to Solomon? *1 Chronicles 28:9*

■ What is the condition of the heart? *Jeremiah 17:9–10*

■ What are we to do above all else? *Proverbs 4:23*

THINK OF SOME OF THE REASONS WHY WE SOMETIMES BECOME PEOPLE PLEASERS.

 Word Study

HYPOCRITE: Hupokritēs – ὑποκριτής (Greek)
A play actor; a stage player who acted under a mask impersonating a character; pretence; a representation of being someone you really are not.

Ministry not Manipulation

Sometimes behind a friendly approach to others there is a desire to manipulate them, to use them to meet our needs. The true motive of reaching towards others is ministry: a desire to give to others, not to get for ourselves.

"Search me, O God, and know my heart; test me and know my anxious thoughts. _____ _____ , and lead me in the way everlasting." Psalm 139:23–24

■ When are we blessed? *Acts 20:35*

■ What are we to take every opportunity to do? *Galatians 6:9–10*

■ What is God pleased with? *Hebrews 13:16*

DISCUSS THE DIFFERENCE BETWEEN MINISTRY AND MANIPULATION.

Facing the Pain

The presence of divine love at the centre of our being spells out joy. The loss of that love spells out pain. Often our relationships reflect the presence of that pain and we adopt a style of relating that protects us from the presence of further pain by keeping people safely distant.

"All a man's ways seem innocent to him, _____ _____ ." Proverbs 16:2

■ How did Jesus handle pain? *Matthew 26:36–46*

■ What has God promised? *Psalm 30:5*

■ What is said of Jesus? *Matthew 12:20*

ILLUSTRATION WHEN A PIECE OF GRIT OR A SMALL STONE ENTERS THE SHELL OF AN OYSTER IT CREATES A WOUND AND PAIN. THE OYSTER SECRETES A SUBSTANCE THAT FORMS AROUND IT AND IT BECOMES A PEARL. PEARLS COME FROM PAIN.

The Need to be Loved

Every one of us longs to be loved and when we fail to experience that love, we hurt and hurt badly. Facing the pain of that deep disappointment helps us to see that there is something in our hearts that no one, not even the most loving human being, can fully satisfy.

"But _____ in this: While we were still sinners, Christ died for us." Romans 5:8

■ What is God's assurance? *Jeremiah 31:3*

■ What is the extent of that love? *Isaiah 53:1–7*

■ How does Isaiah describe the result of restoration? *Isaiah 35*

Action Plan

This week as you relate to people, start to ask yourself the question "Am I ministering to people or am I manipulating them?".

Recap

The Christian quality of love reaches out to others. Often because of deep disappointment and pain we develop a relational style designed to always get a positive response from others. This is a subtle form of manipulation because we are using others to meet our need of value and acceptance. In order to be able to give love to others, we must face the deep pain of rejection we feel and draw on God's love, recognising that no human being can meet the deepest needs of our heart.

Restoring Relationship

Key Truth

"... _____ . He guides me in paths of righteousness for his name's sake." Psalm 23:3

At the heart of God's creation is the theme of relationships. Broken in Adam, restored in Christ, and renewed in the fellowship of the saints: God has done everything possible to restore our relationship to Him, we must do everything possible to restore our relationships with each other.

The Inner Struggle

There is within us a deep down desire to avoid the idea that we are powerless to make our life work on its own. To admit that puts us in a position of helplessness rather than control and we really struggle to come to that place.

" 'I am the vine; you are the branches. If a man remains in me and I in him, he will bear much fruit; _____ .' " John 15:5

■ How did Paul describe this struggle? *Romans 7:15–20*

■ How did he handle his struggle? *Romans 8:1–2 & 9–11*

■ What conclusion does he come to? *Romans 8:35–39*

THINK IN WHAT WAYS DO WE TRY TO CONTROL OUR OWN LIVES?

A Spirit of Independence

Sin is much more than wrong actions, it is a wrong attitude. It is the attitude that displaces God from the centre of our lives and replaces Him with our ego, "a declaration of independence".

" 'But his subjects hated him and sent a delegation after him to say, " _____

_____ ." ' " Luke 19:14

■ What is the shortest definition of sin in the Bible? *Isaiah 14:12–15*

■ What was the issue with the rich young ruler? *Mark 10:17–31*

■ What does God not despise? *Psalm 51:17*

DISCUSS WHAT SIN REALLY IS.

P Practical Tip

Always remember that the ego is at the centre of:

PR **I** DE
S **N**
GU **I** LT

Relational Sin

The ugliness of relational sin lies in the fact that it violates the command to love. Once we realise our sinful self-protection we need to come to God and ask His forgiveness for trying to make our life work on our own.

" 'For whoever wants to save his life _____

_____

for me and for the gospel will save it.' " Mark 8:35

■ What is the principle of the grain of wheat? *John 12:24–26*

■ How did Paul express this? *Philippians 3:4–10*

■ What do we find hard to do? *Proverbs 3:5*

■ What is promised when we trust? *Isaiah 26:3*

DISCUSS WHAT IT MEANS TO LOSE OUR LIFE.

The Path of Repentance

The only way to deal with relational sin is to repent and seek God's forgiveness for violating the law of love and looking to our own interests.

"Return, O Israel, to the Lord your God. _____ !" Hosea 14:1

■ What is said of Israel? *Isaiah 30:15*

■ How did the prodigal son see relational sin? *Luke 15:18*

■ What was the root of it? *Luke 15:11–16*

■ How did he deal with it? *Luke 15:19–24*

PAUSE FOR PRAYER SPEND SOME MOMENTS REPENTING OF THE SPIRIT OF INDEPENDENCE.

Word Study

REPENTANCE: Metanoeō – μετανοέω (Greek)
A complete change of mind that leads to a complete change of direction, that leads to a complete change in behaviour, through submission of the will.

The Fruit of Repentance

When we repent deeply of our sins it enables God to move into our lives with might and power, and releases us to reach out to others in the power and strength of His life and love.

" 'Produce fruit in keeping with _____ .' " Matthew 3:8

■ What accompanies repentance? *2 Corinthians 7:9–10*

■ What is the result of repentance? *Acts 3:19*

■ How is this evidenced? *Luke 15:22*

PAUSE FOR PRAISE INVITE THE HOLY SPIRIT TO COME UPON YOU AFRESH AND SPEND SOME MOMENTS GIVING THANKS TO GOD FOR HIS GREAT MERCY.

Action Plan

Make sure you attend your church's next communion service and partake of the bread and wine. Remind yourself of how much you have been forgiven, that you received mercy when you deserved judgment.

Recap

God wants us to restore relationships, but there is often an inner struggle because of a strong spirit of independence which violates the law of love and leads us into relational sin. We must come and repent of our independence from God and His grace so that He can release us to reach out to others in the power of His endless love.

Living in Relationship

Key Truth

"But if we walk in the light, as he is in the light, _____
_____ , and the blood of
Jesus, his Son, purifies us from all sin." I John 1:7

It is probably the greatest scandal of the universe that the Church, which is designed by God to be the shop window through which the world can look and see what relationships are all about, reflects so poorly the principle of loving as we have been loved. This surely is one of the most critical issues of the day that we face.

Our Great Example

Jesus demonstrated the true heart of love, which as we have seen is moving towards other people without self-protection. He was rejected, despised, vilified and failed by those closest to Him, but He did not withdraw, He kept reaching out.

*"He came to that which was his own, _____
_____ ."* John 1:11

■ Where was Jesus' dependence? *John 5:26–43*

■ Did Jesus resort to self-protection? *Matthew 27:12–14*

■ How did Jesus demonstrate His dependence? *Matthew 26:39–44*

LIST   THE INSTANCES IN THE BIBLE WHEN PEOPLE FAILED JESUS:

E.g. the disciples fell asleep
_____
_____
_____

Face the Facts

If the Church is going to be the core ministry God intended it to be, we must acknowledge that generally speaking the Church is greatly struggling in the area of relationship.

"If you keep on biting and devouring each other, watch out or _____ *."* Galatians 5:15

■ What was Paul concerned about? *1 Corinthians 1:10–11*

■ How did he categorise it? *1 Corinthians 3:3*

■ What is the end result if we don't face the facts? *Luke 11:7*

CHALLENGE HOW IS THE STATE OF RELATIONSHIPS IN YOUR CHURCH OR FELLOWSHIP?

Living in Love

Our ability to reach out to others does not come through greater effort but out of our response to how much we are divinely loved.

" _____ *, because we are convinced that one died for all, and therefore all died."* 2 Corinthians 5:14

■ What did Jesus underline as the key? *John 15:9*

■ What is the result? *John 15:10–11*

■ What is the basis? *John 15:12*

Taking the Risk

There are great risks in relationships, perhaps the biggest one is when we move towards others they respond negatively. When we draw on God's love it enables us to go on loving and taking the risk.

"In the same way, faith by itself, _____ _____ *, is dead."* James 2:17

■ How does Paul describe the painfulness of life experience? *2 Corinthians 4:7–9*

■ Why did he not lose heart? *2 Corinthians 4:16*

■ Where was he focused? *2 Corinthians 4:18*

TALK THROUGH SOME OF THE RISKS WE TAKE WHEN WE REACH OUT TO OTHERS.

Supporting One Another

God has not created us as independent islands. We need the help of each other to see the subterfuges and camouflages that go on in our personalities. Our brothers and sisters help us to see and face specific issues.

"_____ _daily, as long as it is called Today, so that none of you may be hardened by sin's deceitfulness._" Hebrews 3:13

■ What are we to do? *Hebrews 10:25*

■ What are the relational implications? *Hebrews 10:24*

■ Why is meeting together important? *James 5:16*

■ Why did the psalmist rejoice? *Psalm 122:1*

LIST SOME OF THE AREAS IN YOUR RELATIONSHIPS YOU HAVE BECOME AWARE OF AS YOU HAVE SHARED IN THIS GROUP

An Expression of God's Love

We are the tangible outworking of God's love to each other. Together we can make the invisible God more real to each other through that experiential awareness of His love. Seeing this makes relating to others a delight not a duty.

"_No-one has ever seen God; but _____ _____ and his love is made complete in us._" 1 John 4:12

■ What is the tangible evidence of God's love? *John 1:14*

■ How is God's glory revealed? *Colossians 1:27*

■ How are we to love one another? *1 Peter 1:22*

■ What is a danger we can fall into? *James 2:1–9*

THINK THROUGH SOME TANGIBLE EXPRESSIONS OF GOD'S LOVE THAT WE CAN DEMONSTRATE:

E.g.   send a card   _____

make a phone call   _____

make a gift   _____

The Place of Blessing

When we give up our position of self-protection and focus on God's great love, a deep awareness of how much we are loved dawns on our soul. We do not want anything from others, we love and that blesses them.

"How good and pleasant it is _____ *!"* Psalm 133:1

■ What are we to make every effort to do? *Ephesians 4:3*

■ How are we to stand and contend for the faith? *Philippians 1:27*

■ How are we to walk? *1 John 1:7*

Action Plan

Following the principle of encouraging one another daily, think of seven different ways you can encourage seven different people during the next seven days.

Recap

God has called us to live in relationships, and Christ is our greatest example. We must face the fact that the Church is struggling in this area, and each of us must draw on God's love and take the risk of loving others even when they hurt us. We need to support each other in this and allow ourselves to be a tangible outworking of His love.

Final Thoughts

This study brings great challenge to our lives. What are some of the challenges you have had to face?

_____

_____

_____

Spend some moments in prayer, asking God to give you the strength and courage to face and follow through on every challenge.

Into Battle

🔑 Key Truth

"For our struggle is not against flesh and blood, but against the rulers, against the authorities, _____

_____

_____ ." Ephesians 6:12

All those who have committed their lives to Jesus Christ know that there are in existence two orders and two kingdoms, the forces of which are locked together in mortal combat. One is the kingdom of God and the other is the kingdom of the devil and Christians, whether they like it or not, are thrust onto the cutting edge of that conflict.

List the characteristics of:

The kingdom of light	The kingdom of darkness

■ What are the three arenas of battle? *1 John 5:4; Galatians 5:17; 1 Peter 5:8*

Discuss THESE THREE ARENAS OF WARFARE AND IDENTIFY SOME OF THE BATTLES THAT WE FACE IN EACH ONE:

_____   _____

_____   _____

_____   _____

_____   _____

Find AT LEAST TEN OF THE DESCRIPTIVE TITLES OF SATAN IN THE BIBLE, E.G., DECEIVER; LIAR

 ## Word Study

DEVIL: Diabolos – διάβολος (Greek)
An accuser; a slanderer, a false accuser; a divider of people, one who casts either himself or something else between two in order to separate them.

SATAN: Satanas – Σατανᾶς (Greek)
An adversary; the opposer; the prince of fallen angels.

A Call to Arms

Many Christians are pacifists when it comes to the matter of earthly warfare, but no one can be a pacifist when it comes to the matter of spiritual warfare. We have been enlisted in the army of God.

_"Timothy, my son, I give you this instruction in keeping with the prophecies once made about you, _____
_____.."_ 1 Timothy 1:18

■ What does Paul say about our weapons of warfare? _2 Corinthians 10:3–5_

■ What are they able to do? _2 Corinthians 10:3–5_

■ What was Paul's charge to Timothy? _1 Timothy 6:12_

Talk through SOME OF THE THINGS THAT ARE REQUIRED WHEN A SOLDIER ENLISTS.

Our Only Protection

The armour of God is our only protection against the wiles of Satan, and it will do us no good unless we avail ourselves of it in its entirety.

"_____ so that you can take your stand against the devil's schemes." Ephesians 6:11

■ What was Paul's advice to Timothy? 2 Timothy 2:3–4

■ What are we to put on? Romans 13:12

 Practical Tip

Armour is good and necessary for protection, but you can only conquer when you have a weapon and know how to use it.

The Belt of Truth

Girding our waist with truth is always the place to start because the first line of attack is always to present lies.

"_____ ; get wisdom, discipline and understanding." Proverbs 23:23

■ What is the cause of sin? Genesis 3:2–4

■ How did Jesus describe it? John 8:42–44

■ Why is truth so crucial? John 8:32

THINK OF SOME OF THE LIES SATAN USES IN HIS ATTACKS.

The Power and Importance of Truth

Because Satan is the arch deceiver he seeks to trick us, but with the belt of truth his deceiving tricks are exposed.

"Surely _____ ; you teach me wisdom in the inmost place." Psalm 51:6

■ What did the psalmist affirm? Psalm 119:11

■ What is an activity of Satan? Revelation 20:3

- How did Satan try to twist the truth? *Matthew 4:6–7*

- Where does Satan seek to begin? *1 John 1:8*

Forms of Dishonesty

Although we outwardly ascribe to truth, we can inwardly resist the truth by subtle defences that must be recognised. Satan uses these to deceive us and only the truth will expose his wiles.

"... ' _____, and I ate.' "
Genesis 3:13b

- PROJECTION – Where is this first seen? How? *Genesis 3:12–13*

- DENIAL – Where does it start? *Mark 14:66–70, Jeremiah 17:9*

- RATIONALISATION – How did Jesus illustrate this? *Matthew 7:3–5*

SHARE TOGETHER HOW SATAN USES THESE SUBTLE PLOYS TO TRICK AND TRAP US.

Action Plan

During this coming week seek to identify some situations where you recognise the use of the three defences mentioned. Look at your own life first, before looking at the lives of others.

Recap

We are engaged in a battle of two kingdoms and have been called to arms. God has made available to us armour for protection, the key piece being the belt of truth. Satan's first attack on the human race was to deceive by lies. It's only truth that can expose his subtle lying strategies.

The Breastplate of Righteousness

Key Truth

"... with the breastplate of righteousness in place ... "
Ephesians 6:14b

We now look at the second piece of armour with which we are able to defend ourselves against the wiles of the devil.

TALK THROUGH HOW YOU GOT ON WITH YOUR ACTION PLAN AND HOW ALERT YOU HAVE BECOME TO SATAN'S LYING TACTICS.

Protects the Heart

Because the breastplate covered mainly the heart, which is the seat of our emotions, this part of the armour protects us from negative and desolating feelings.

"*Above all else, _____*

_____ ." Proverbs 4:23

■ What is the heart? *Proverbs 4:23*

■ What did Jesus say about the potential of the heart? *Mark 7:21–23*

■ How did Jesus link the heart to behaviour? *Matthew 5:27–28*

Word Study

HEART: Kardia – καρδία (Greek)
The chief organ of physical life. The word came to stand for man's entire mental and moral activity, both the rational and emotional elements – used figuratively for the hidden springs of the personal life.

Not Good Enough

Our own righteousness is flawed, but Christ's righteousness is impenetrable, because Satan can find no fault in Him. When we stand in His righteousness our protection is secure.

"Christ is the end of the law so that _____
_____ *."* Romans 10:4

■ What is our righteousness like? *Isaiah 64:6*

■ What did Paul declare? *Philippians 3:9*

■ What feeling does this enable us to withstand? *Romans 8:1*

Word Study

RIGHTEOUSNESS:
Dikaiosunē – δικαιοσύνη (Greek)
The character or quality of being right or just, standing the test of God's judgment; conformity to the standards of God's character.

DISCUSS THE DIFFERENCE BETWEEN SELF-RIGHTEOUSNESS AND GOD'S RIGHTEOUSNESS, AND SATAN'S STRATEGY IN RELATIONSHIP TO THEM.

I Must be Perfect

Some people carry the feeling that they are only accepted by God when they are doing everything perfectly. They carry a feeling of never doing enough to be thought well of by God.

*"_____ ,
_____ but I press on to take hold of that for which Christ Jesus took hold of me."* Philippians 3:12

■ What kind of people does God choose? *1 Corinthians 1:28–29*

■ How is God's power made perfect? *2 Corinthians 12:9*

 Practical Tip

Change your last name to Arnott, e.g. John Arnott. Now read I Corinthians 1:28–29 again. Hallelujah!

Discouragement through Criticism

Satan can often use others to attack us with criticism, but when we wear the breastplate of righteousness we do not need to defend ourselves by attacking back.

"For I am the least of the apostles and do not even deserve to be called an apostle, _____

_____ ." 1 Corinthians 15:9

■ What was Jesus willing to do? *Philippians 2:7*

■ How did He deal with criticism? *Matthew 27:12–14*

■ To what point did threats and criticism bring Elijah to? *1 Kings 19:1–4*

List some elements of:

Destructive criticism	Constructive criticism

Confusion

Confusion comes when we have no clear answer or understanding and Satan rides in to bring doubt and despair. Confidence in the righteous justice of a holy God causes us to withstand any such attack and remain in His peace.

"_____

_____, but of peace, as in all churches of the saints." 1 Corinthians 14:33 (AV)

■ Where does peace stem from? *Isaiah 26:3*

■ What does the peace of God do? *Philippians 4:7*

■ What brings instability? *James 1:8*

Does God Love Me?

Another feeling which the devil delights to arouse in an unprotected and unguarded heart is the feeling that God does not love us, especially when things seem to be going wrong.

"He replied, 'I have been very zealous for the Lord God Almighty. The Israelites have rejected your covenant, broken down your altars, and put your prophets to death with the sword.

_____

_____ .' " 1 Kings 19:10

■ What did Paul focus back on to reaffirm God's love? *Ephesians 2:3–5*

■ What did Paul pray for the Ephesians? *Ephesians 3:17–19*

■ What did he affirm to them? *Ephesians 3:20*

SPEND A FEW MOMENTS GIVING THANKS TO GOD FOR HIS BLESSINGS AND GOODNESS TO YOU.

Failure

In moments of failure the adversary accuses us and condemns us. With a penitent heart, through forgiveness, we can put on again the breastplate of righteousness.

"

_____

_____

and purify us from all unrighteousness." 1 John 1:9

■ What action are we to take? *Isaiah 55:6–7*

■ What promise are we to embrace? *Isaiah 43:25*

■ What is the result? *Isaiah 1:18–20*

Action Plan

Each morning when you get up focus on God's justice and mercy, and then visualise yourself wearing the breastplate. Visualise the six arrows mentioned bouncing off.

Recap

When the breastplate of righteousness is in place our hearts are protected. Satan attacks the heart with condemnation, accusations, worthlessness and discouragement through criticism and confusion. As our confidence is in God's justice and righteous dealings, even when things go wrong and we fail we can again pick up the breastplate of righteousness.

A Firm Footing

Key Truth

"... _____

_____ that comes from the gospel of peace." Ephesians 6:15

Shoes are absolutely essential to the soldier. He could not effectively engage in battle without them, as they gave him a firm stance and prevented him from slipping and sliding.

SHARE HOW YOU GOT ON WITH YOUR ACTION PLAN.

Solid Footing

The New English Bible puts it this way: "... let the shoes on your feet be the gospel of peace, to give you firm footing."

" _____

_____,

but the wicked will be silenced in darkness." 1 Samuel 2:9a

■ How can feet be beautiful? _Isaiah 52:7_

■ What was David able to testify? _Psalm 40:2_

■ What did the psalmist praise God for? _Psalm 66:8–9_

THINK WHAT ARE SOME OF THE WAYS OUR FEET CAN OFTEN STEP?

Stand Firm on Foundational Truths

When under attack from the wiles of the devil we need to stand firm on the truth of the Gospel.

_"Whatever happens, conduct yourselves in a manner worthy of the gospel of Christ. Then, whether I come and see you or only hear about you in my absence, _____

_____ in one spirit, contending as one man for the faith of the gospel ..."_ Philippians 1:27

- What did Paul want his Philippian friends to do? *Philippians 4:1*

- What encouraged Paul? *1 Thessalonians 3:7–8*

- What was Paul's instruction to Timothy? *2 Timothy 2:15*

LIST WHAT YOU CONSIDER TO BE SOME OF THE FOUNDATIONAL TRUTHS (WORK IN PAIRS):

_____

_____

_____

_____

Choose to Stand

You cannot stand until you are prepared to stand. It begins with a firm and resolute attitude which then issues in firm and resolute action.

"So then, brothers, _____ _____ , whether by word of mouth or by letter." 2 Thessalonians 2:15

- What was the challenge to the Children of Israel? *Deuteronomy 30:19*

- What brings instability? *James 1:8*

- What did Paul exhort the Corinthians to do? *1 Corinthians 15:58*

- What are we to be and do? *1 Peter 5:8–9*

DISCUSS SOME OF THE AREAS WHERE WE NEED TO STAND AND RESIST.

Peace that Does Not Go to Pieces

As Christians we have an advantage over every other soldier, we have inside information. We may not win every skirmish but we win the war. If you have peace about the outcome, you will have peace all the way.

"_____,
since as members of one body you were called to peace. And be thankful." Colossians 3:15

■ What is the kingdom of God? *Romans 14:17*

■ What are we to take heart about? *John 16:33*

■ What does this bring? *Psalm 29:11*

■ What does the peace of God do? *Philippians 4:7*

 Practical Tip
Remember, peace is not the absence of conflict, it is the inner poise and tranquillity to be experienced when conflict is going on all around you.

The Shield of Faith

The main purpose of the shield in Roman times was to protect from the fiery darts thrown by the enemy.

"*... for everyone born of God overcomes the world.* _____

_____ ." 1 John 5:4

■ What did Paul exhort Timothy to do?
1 Timothy 1:18–19

■ What had some discarded? *1 Timothy 1:19*

■ What was the result? *1 Timothy 1:19*

WRITE OUT YOUR OWN DEFINITION OF FAITH.

Faith is _____

_____

_____

SHARE YOUR DEFINITION WITH THE GROUP.

Fiery Darts

"But the Lord stood at my side and gave me strength, so that through me the message might be fully proclaimed and all the Gentiles might hear it. _____

_____ ." 2 Timothy 4:17

■ What was Paul's concern? *2 Corinthians 11:3*

■ What do we accomplish by using our weapons?
2 Corinthians 10:4

■ Where should we bring every thought?
2 Corinthians 10:5

■ What is the result of a steadfast mind? *Isaiah 26:3*

THINK OF OTHER BIBLE PASSAGES THAT ADDRESS THE MIND.

Action Plan

Take three of the foundational truths you have listed and this week find another Christian to sit down with and in 20 minutes explain them clearly to them.

Recap

We must take a resolute stand, experiencing the peace of God in the thick of the battle, standing firm on the foundational truths which provide a solid footing. As we take the shield of faith, the lying thoughts of Satan are exposed and parried.

The Helmet of Salvation

 Key Truth
"Take the helmet of salvation ... " Ephesians 6:17a

Just as the breastplate of righteousness protects us from emotional distress, so the helmet protects us from mental distress, and keeps our thinking straight.

HOW DID YOU GET ON WITH YOUR ACTION PLAN?

A Stayed Mind

There has never been a time in history when the mind has been so bombarded every moment of the day as now. We need continual protection in the battle for the mind.

"You will keep in perfect peace him _____ _____ , because he trusts in you." Isaiah 26:3

■ What did Paul write to the Ephesians? *Ephesians 4:17–24*

■ What does Paul contrast? *Romans 8:5–7*

SCRIPTURE SEARCH FIND TEN DIFFERENT DESCRIPTIONS OF THE MIND FROM SCRIPTURE. LIST WITH THE REFERENCE:

E.g.   right mind *Mark 5:15*
corrupt mind *1 Timothy 6:5*

DISCUSS WHAT THESE WORDS MEAN.

Salvation

It is important to recognise that Paul is not just talking about salvation from sin, but salvation in its entirety, past, present and future.

"*But since we belong to the day, let us be self-controlled, putting on faith and love as a breastplate, _____*

_____ *.*" 1 Thessalonians 5:8

■ What did David affirm? *Psalm 27:1–6*
In what context did he express it?

■ What are we to continually work out?
Philippians 2:12

DISCUSS WHAT THIS MEANS AND LIST SOME THINGS WE NEED TO BE CONTINUALLY SAVED FROM, AS WELL AS SIN.

E.g.   ourselves
temptation

God's Eternal Plan

The helmet of salvation protects us from the doom, gloom and pessimism of a world destroying itself. The kingdom of God will be established and creation will be delivered from its bondage.

"_____ .

But hope that is seen is not hope at all. Who hopes for what he already has?" Romans 8:24

■ What is the whole of creation doing?
Romans 8:22

■ What does creation wait for? *Romans 8:18–21*

■ Why do we have strong hope? *Hebrews 12:2; Revelation 1:8*

DISCUSS TOGETHER THE MEANING OF ECCLESIASTES 3:11

Take Heart

The helmet of salvation is the recognition that all human schemes, all human disorders and all human chaos will one day be ended, and it will be seen that God has been quietly working His purposes out. Take courage.

" 'I have told you these things, so that in me you may have peace. In this world you will have trouble. _____ _____ .' " John 16:33

■ What is necessary in battle? *Joshua 1:6*

■ What did Paul admonish the Corinthians about? *1 Corinthians 16:13*

■ What are we to hold on to? *Hebrews 3:6*

Hope in a Hopeless World

What does a Christian do when he feels helpless to end wars and strife and change governments? It is only in the strength of the hope of the day of salvation that our hearts and minds can be kept undisturbed.

" _____ _____, *firm and secure. It enters the inner sanctuary behind the curtain* ..." Hebrews 6:19

■ What have we been born into? *1 Peter 1:3*

■ How were we once? *Ephesians 2:12*

■ How did the psalmist talk to himself? *Psalm 42:5*

Word Study

HOPE: Elpis – ἐλπίς (Greek)
A favourable and confident expectation;
a positive assurance.

THINK THROUGH AND LIST TEN REASONS WHY
WE HAVE HOPE.

E.g.   we are saved
         we trust God's Word

Action Plan

Memorise Psalm 42:5

Recap

When we put on the helmet of salvation it protects our minds. It enables us to see the eternal perspective in a hopeless world, protecting us from gloom and pessimism, knowing that we have been saved, are being saved and will be saved.

A Powerful Weapon

Key Truth

**"... and the sword of the Spirit, which is the word of God."
Ephesians 6:17b**

John Stott points out that "of all the six pieces of armour or weaponry listed, the sword is the only one that can be used for attack as well as defence".

SEE HOW MANY IN THE GROUP CAN RECITE PSALM 42:5 FROM MEMORY.

Resist the Devil

We are right when we develop a healthy respect for the devil's wiles and ingenuity, but we are wrong when we allow him to terrorise and frighten us.

"*Submit yourselves, then, to God. _____
_____ .*" James 4:7

■ What are we not to let the devil gain? *Ephesians 4:27*

■ Is the devil a roaring lion? *1 Peter 5:8–9*

THINK THROUGH WHAT ARE SOME OF THE FOOTHOLDS SATAN SEEKS TO ESTABLISH?

The Power of the Word

Jesus, who had embraced the written Word, made sure that it became the spoken Word as He rebutted the attack of Satan.

"*Jesus answered, 'It is written: "Man does not live on bread alone,_____
_____ ." ' "* Matthew 4:4

■ How is the Word of God described? *Hebrews 4:12*

■ How did they overcome the accuser? *Revelation 12:11*

■ What did Jesus declare? *John 6:63*

An Inspired Book

The Bible is not merely a human document, the product of the mind of Man. The Holy Spirit breathed into men and inspired them to write it the way it is.

"But when he, the Spirit of truth, comes, _____ . He will not speak on his own; he will speak only what he hears, and he will tell you what is yet to come." John 16:13

■ What did Paul write to the Colossians? *Colossians 3:16*

■ Where must God's Word be written? *Hebrews 10:15–16*

■ What did Paul confirm to Timothy? *2 Timothy 3:16*

ACTIVITY GO ROUND THE GROUP QUOTING MEMORY VERSES – SEE HOW MANY YOU CAN QUOTE.

 Practical Tip

When seeking to memorise Scripture, start by memorising the key words first.

A Work of the Holy Spirit

Only the Holy Spirit can show us how to use the Word. Remember it is not your sword but "the sword of the Spirit".

"_____ does not accept the things that come from the Spirit of God, for they are foolishness to him, and he cannot understand them, because they are spiritually discerned." 1 Corinthians 2:14

 Word Study

INSPIRATION:
Theopneustos – θεόπνευστος (Greek)
Breathed out by God; carried along by the truth of the Spirit.

■ What title did Jesus give the Holy Spirit?
John 14:16–17

■ What happens when we use the Word as **our** sword?
2 Corinthians 3:6

List some:

Wrong uses of the Word	Right uses of the Word

E.g.   to condemn
       to hurt
       legalistically
	E.g. to encourage
	       to heal
	       to minister grace

Divine Teacher

When we allow the Holy Spirit to teach us the truth it takes root within us, and whenever we stand in need of a word to rebuke the devil the Holy Spirit brings it to remembrance.

"But the Counsellor, the Holy Spirit, whom the Father will send in my name, will teach you all things _____

_____

_____ *."* John 14:26

■ What did Jesus say of the Holy Spirit?
John 16:13

■ What did Jesus promise? *Luke 12:11–12*

Truth Alone

When it comes to the matter of defeating Satan, we do not need knowledge of science, philosophy, politics, or the arts: the Word alone has within it the power of his destruction.

"For the word of God is living and active. _____

_____

_____ , joints and marrow; it judges the thoughts and attitudes of the heart." Hebrews 4:12

■ What can God's Word become in our mouths? *Jeremiah 5:14, 23:29*

■ What did the psalmist testify? *Psalm 119:103, 105*

■ What does truth expose? *John 3:19–21*

QUOTE D. L. MOODY SAID, "IF A STICK IS CROOKED YOU DON'T HAVE TO SHOUT LOUDLY ABOUT IT, JUST LAY A STRAIGHT ONE ALONGSIDE IT."

Know the Truth

If we are to conquer Satan in the same way that Jesus did we must know the Bible in its entirety. You must quote it to him and quote it precisely.

" 'Sanctify them by the truth; _____

_____ .' " John 17:17

■ How was Timothy to use the truth? *2 Timothy 2:15*

■ When does the truth set us free? *John 8:32*

■ What is said of the Bereans? *Acts 17:11*

Action Plan

This week begin to commit to memory the passage that these studies focus on – *Ephesians 6:12–18.*

Recap

We can resist the devil through the power of the Word, which is inspired by the Holy Spirit, who guides us into all truth. As we come to know that truth, and the Holy Spirit uses it through us, it is all we need to defeat our adversary.

Watch and Pray

Key Truth

"And pray in the Spirit on all occasions with all kinds of prayers and requests. With this in mind, _____

_____ for all the saints." Ephesians 6:18

Having examined the six pieces of armour, it is not sufficient to stop there. In this our final week of the studies, we must look at a last key element: unless the armour is worn by a *praying* Christian it will not be an effective defence.

HOW DID YOU GET ON WITH YOUR ACTION PLAN? HOW MUCH OF THE PASSAGE ON THE ARMOUR OF GOD HAVE YOU COMMITTED TO MEMORY?

Praying Always

Praying in the Spirit is something that ought to pervade all our spiritual warfare and is something we have to do, and keep on doing, if we are to win the battle against Satan and his forces.

" ' _____

_____ ,

_____ *and that you may be able to stand before the Son of Man.' "* Luke 21:36

■ What did Jesus teach in this parable? *Luke 18:1–8*

■ What was Paul's desire? *1 Timothy 2:8*

DISCUSS THE IMPLICATIONS OF THE FOUR 'ALLS' IN EPHESIANS 6:18

A Vital Relationship

A soldier cannot fight independently, he must be part of an army and be in close relationship with his commander, following his instructions.

" 'This, then, is how you should pray: " _____
_____, hallowed be your name." ' " Matthew 6:9

◼ What does this verse reveal? *Matthew 3:17*

◼ What was the key to Jesus' ministry? *John 8:28–29*

◼ How did Jesus nurture His relationship? *Matthew 14:23*

 Practical Tip
Remember, you can only effectively wield authority when you yourself are under authority.

Vigilant Prayer

In the midst of the battle it is possible to so focus on the enemy that we neglect to be vigilant and constant in prayer.

" _____
_____
and thankful." Colossians 4:2

◼ What is the antidote for battle anxiety? *Philippians 4:6*

◼ What needs to accompany prayer? *Colossians 4:2*

◼ How often should we pray? *1 Thessalonians 5:17*

LIST THE DIFFERENT WAYS OF PRAYING AND DISCUSS THEM.

E.g. verbal prayer; silent prayer; group prayer

Praying in the Spirit

This is prayer that is prompted and guided by the Holy Spirit.

*"In the same way, the Spirit helps us in our weakness. We do not know what we ought to pray for, _____
_____
with groans that words cannot express."* Romans 8:26

◼ What are we to do? *Galatians 5:25*

◼ What is Jude's exhortation? *Jude verse 20*

◼ What differentiation did Paul make?
1 Corinthians 14:15

Praying with Liberty

There is hardly anything more wonderful in the Christian life than to experience liberty and freedom in prayer. Satan has no hold on us there.

" 'The Spirit gives life; the flesh counts for nothing. _____

_____

_____ .' " John 6:63

■ What does the Spirit of the Lord bring? *2 Corinthians 3:17*

■ How are we not to pray? *Matthew 6:7*

■ What sets us free? *Romans 8:2*

STOP AND PRAY SPEND A FEW MOMENTS ASKING THE HOLY SPIRIT TO COME UPON YOU AFRESH. SING TOGETHER THE CHORUS, "BREATHE ON ME BREATH OF GOD".

Praying for the Saints

Each soldier in an army must have the good of his fellow soldiers at heart. They are in the battle together, and must stick together and support one another.

"And pray in the Spirit on all occasions with all kinds of prayers and requests. With this in mind, be alert and _____

_____ ." Ephesians 6:18

■ What pattern was set for us? *John 17:20*

■ How was this reinforced? *Romans 1:9; Ephesians 1:16, 3:16; Philippians 1:4; Colossians 1:3*

THINK OF SOME OF THE CHRISTIANS YOU KNOW WHO ARE STRUGGLING AND GET THE GROUP TO PRAY FOR THEM.

Pray for Me

We need to be humble enough to ask our brothers and sisters to pray for us in the heart of the battle.

" _____ ." 1 Thessalonians 5:25

■ What did Paul urge? *Romans 15:30*

■ What were Paul's prayer requests? *2 Thessalonians 3:1–2*

■ Break down into twos and pray for each other.

Spiritual Victory

As we take all of the armour of God and move forward praying in the Spirit continuously and fervently, the enemy of our souls will be routed.

"For our struggle is not against flesh and blood, but against the rulers, against the authorities, against the powers of this dark world and against the _____

_____*."* Ephesians 6:12

■ What has Jesus invested in us? *Luke 10:19*

■ What was Paul convinced of? *Romans 8:38–39*
Why? *Romans 8:37*

SING TOGETHER THE GRAHAM KENDRICK SONG "FOR THIS PURPOSE CHRIST WAS REVEALED".

Action Plan

Every day this week, when you get up in the morning, spend some moments in prayer putting your armour on. As you pray, see yourself putting the pieces on, as if you were looking in the mirror.

Recap

Having put the armour on, our relationship to the Lord must be maintained and strengthened through vigilant prayer in the Spirit for the saints, whilst also recognising our own need of prayer from our brothers and sisters. As we move forward in battle we can anticipate and expect victory.

Final Thoughts

Look back over the six studies and list the three most important things you have got out of them:

_____

_____

_____

Spend a few minutes in a prayer of re-enlistment in the army of the Lord and then go out and do battle for the kingdom of God!

CWR, Waverley Abbey House, Waverley Lane, Farnham, Surrey GU9 8EP

NATIONAL DISTRIBUTORS

Australia
Christian Marketing Pty Ltd., PO Box 154, North Geelong,
Victoria 3215 Tel: (052) 786100

Canada
Christian Marketing Canada Ltd., PO Box 7000, Niagara on the Lake,
Ontario LOS 1JO Tel: 416 641 0631

Malaysia
Salvation Book Centre (M), 23 Jalan SS2/64,
Sea Park, 47300 Petaling Jaya, Selangor

Nigeria
FBFM, No 2 Mbu Close, S/W Ikoyi, Lagos, Nigeria
Tel: (01) 611 160

Republic of Ireland
Scripture Union, 40 Talbot Street, Dublin 1
Tel: 363764

Singapore
Alby Commercial Enterprises Pte. Ltd., 8 Kaki Bukit Road 2,
Ruby Warehouse Complex, No 04-38, Singapore 1441
Tel: 65 741 0411

Southern Africa
Struick Christian Books (Pty Ltd), PO Box 193, Maitland 7405,
Cape Town, South Africa
Tel: (021) 551 1124

Text © 1993 by Trevor J Partridge

This edition © 1993 CWR

Printed in Great Britain by Dowland Press

Design and Typesetting: CWR Design & Production

Photos © Creative Publishing

ISBN 1-85345-070-7

All rights reserved. No part of this publication may be reproduced, stored in a retrieval system, or transmitted, in any form or by any means, electronic, mechanical, photocopying, recording or otherwise, without the prior permission in writing of CWR.

Unless otherwise identified, all Scripture quotations in this publication are from the Holy Bible: New International Version (NIV). Copyright © 1973, 1978, 1984, International Bible Society.